presents

BIG STIX

The Greatest Hitters in the History of the Major Leagues

Rob Rains

www.sportspublishingllc.com

Sports Publishing L.L.C.
Authorized licensee of Rawlings Sporting Goods Company, Inc.®

Rawlings® is a trademark of Rawlings Sporting Goods Company, Inc.®
Rawlings trademarks and copyrights are used with the permission of
Rawlings Sporting Goods Company, Inc.®

The views expressed in this book are those of the author and do not
necessarily reflect those of Rawlings Sporting Goods Company, Inc.®

Director of production: Susan M. Moyer
Acquisitions editor: Bob Snodgrass
Developmental editor: Kipp Wilfong
Book design, senior project manager: Jennifer L. Polson
Dust jacket design: Joseph Brumleve
Imaging: Christine F. Mohrbacher
Copy editor: Cynthia L. McNew
Photo editor: Erin Linden-Levy

ISBN: 1-58261-757-0

Printed in Canada

Sports Publishing L.L.C.
Visit us online at www.sportspublishingllc.com

Contents

Acknowledgments

The author would like to thank several people who made this book possible, including Mickey Bell and Tim Richards of Rawlings® and Kipp Wilfong and Bob Snodgrass of Sports Publishing.

Thanks as well to Bret Blanchard at Equity Management for his help throughout this project.

Introduction

Many books have been published over the years trying to answer a simple question—who are the best baseball players in the history of the game?

As simple as that question is, there is no simple answer. If there was a simple answer, we would all agree on it and there would be no reason to debate it or look any further for new information that either supports or refutes our opinions or the opinions of others.

With the proliferation of computers and statistical analysis in recent years, more studies have been done that "scientifically" prove a particular player was the best ever. Basically, you feed all of the statistics you want to include into a computer and let that machine spit out the answer about who was the best ever, according to the data you submitted.

Other books have answered that question with opinions, either the personal viewpoint of the writer, or by interviewing players, coaches, managers and others associated with the game and compiling a list.

Both of these systems are interesting, but not without fault. In truth, there is no way to accurately rank the best players in the history of the game. Far too many variables exist, running the gamut from differences in the ballparks, to different eras in history, to different equipment, to different playing conditions—the list goes on and on. Some studies have tried to come up with a computer format that takes all of those factors into account in ranking players, but who truly knows how to accurately weigh those factors?

It seems there is a statistic in baseball for everything these days, and sometimes the game has become so weighted down by the use of those statistics that you tend to forget the fundamental skills of the game—hitting, pitching and fielding.

This book is limited to only one of those dimensions of the game—hitting. It is another attempt to rank the greatest hitters in the history of the game, but it differs from many of the earlier attempts in a couple of major ways.

First, no opinion is involved, either of the writer or from any other source. Second, the statistics used to rank the hitters are among the most basic statistics that have been kept since the game was invented. There was no attempt to "weight" the statistics with reference to ballpark factors or lively ball vs. dead ball, etc. The numbers speak for themselves.

The belief here is that there are too many statistics in baseball and that the game is at its best in its purest, simplest form. Thus when the decision was made about how many and which categories to use for this study, the list was limited to six—hits, RBIs, home runs, doubles, triples and total bases. Those categories combine to form this part of the essence of the game—hitting.

Other categories were considered, but not included for a variety of reasons. Runs, for example, are often a product of someone else's accomplishment. The only time a hitter can account for his own run is when he hits a home run, and that category is included. Slugging percentage and on-base percentage were also considered and discarded, for similar reasons. It seemed that by already using doubles, triples, home runs and total bases, that part of a hitter's game was already being measured. The only additional category that would have been included by using on-base percentage was walks, and that is more of a reflection on the pitcher's performance than on the hitter.

Thus the decision was made to limit the study to those six categories. The rankings were determined by listing the top 25 hitters of all time in each of the various categories. Points were then awarded based on where a hitter ranked in each category. The hitter who ranked at the top of a particular category received 25 points; the person who ranked 25th received one point.

The totals for each category were then added together to come up with a total score. The top 25 hitters of all time, using these rankings, are those who received the greatest number of total points.

Obviously to be successful in these rankings, a hitter had to succeed at more than one element of the game. Hitters who have more than 500 home runs, for example, but do not rank in the top 25 in any other category did not make this list—even though many would consider them among the greatest hitters in the history of the game.

No preference was given to when a player played—a hitter who recorded 3,000 career hits before 1920 received just as much credit for those hits as a player who played in the 1980s and 1990s. There also was no preference given to any player who missed time while serving in the military, with one exception.

Ted Williams is considered one of the greatest hitters in the history of the game, but ranks only 24th on this list. The reason is obvious—he missed three years of his career to serve in the military during World War II and the Korean War. Because this study is based on career numbers, his numbers are lower than many players because of all of the games he missed.

Williams's numbers were broken down a little further, to reveal his "average" performance during a game, then multiplied to include the games he could have played had he not missed the three years while in the military. The conclusion—if Williams had played those three seasons and performed at the same pace as he did for the rest of his career, he would have edged out Hank Aaron as the greatest hitter in history.

Disagree with the choice of categories if you like—part of the beauty of baseball is the diverse opinions of the game's fans—but you can't disagree with the numbers. Using these six categories, the hitters included in this book are the top 25 in the history of the game.

The same categories were used to also rank the top five active hitters in the game and the top five hitters in the history of the World Series. The postseason was not used for obvious reasons—there are so many extra playoff games now that the players who appeared in the major leagues prior to 1969 did not have a chance to play that including those games would produce unfair results.

Because two of the top five active hitters also are ranked in the top 25 in the history of the game, the active list was expanded to include the next five after Barry Bonds and Rafael Palmeiro. For the active and World Series lists, the rankings were based on the top 10 hitters in each category. Points were awarded on a 10-to-1 scale and added to produce the results. Interestingly, the top five World Series hitters are all members of the New York Yankees.

Is this a perfect system? No. Is there a perfect system? No. Selecting the greatest hitters of all time is a simple question without a simple answer.

BIG STIX

THE GREATEST HITTERS IN THE HISTORY OF THE MAJOR LEAGUES

No. 1
Hank Aaron

The one statistic that even the most casual baseball fan knows about Hank Aaron is that he hit 755 home runs during his career, breaking what had been the record of 714 set by Babe Ruth.

If that is all they know, however, they are doing Aaron a tremendous disservice. He was much more than a home run hitter and deserves to be remembered and recognized for all of his accomplishments in baseball, which went far beyond the home run record.

The Rawlings ranking is one way of giving Aaron his due as the greatest hitter, not just home run hitter, in the history of the game.

Aaron ranks on top of the Rawlings scales with 115 points, three more than Ty Cobb. Not only is he the all-time leader in home runs, he is also number one in RBIs, number one in total bases, third all-time in career hits and ninth all-time in career doubles.

"The best thing you can say about him is, when you walk on the field and you're playing against Hank Aaron, you are in the big leagues," Pete Rose once said.

Aaron did not give many indications that he was going to be such a star when he first began to play baseball. He did not play the sport in high school, but played semipro when he was as young as 15. He began his true professional career at the age of 18, signing with the Indianapolis Clowns of the Negro League in 1952.

He was a shortstop then, and he hit with a crosshanded grip—nobody had taught him the proper way to hold a bat. He also hit off his front foot, saying he had learned to hit that way growing up in Mobile, Alabama, trying to swat bottle caps with a broomstick.

"A bottle cap will change direction in an instant," Aaron once said. "You had to be ready."

A scout for the Boston Braves saw enough talent in Aaron that he signed him to a contract with a $7,500 bonus. Aaron thus became the last Negro League player to make the jump to the major leagues. In his first at-bat in spring training in 1954, he hit a long home run over a row of trailers against Boston pitcher Ike Delock that prompted Ted Williams to inquire about Aaron and where he had come from.

A broken ankle suffered that spring by Bobby Thomson opened a spot in the outfield of the Braves—who had moved to Milwaukee—and Aaron capitalized on the chance and never looked back. He hit his first career homer on April 23, 1954, off the Cardinals' Vic Raschi in St. Louis, and finished his rookie season with solid numbers of 13 homers, 69 RBIs and a .280 average.

Aaron had such an easygoing approach that he made the game look simple, but he was serious about what he was doing. He once was asked why he didn't smile more when he was on the field, and Aaron's reply was that he wasn't on the field to have fun; he was there to do a job.

OPPOSITE: The Milwaukee Braves' Hank Aaron slugs his way to first base. (John G. Zimmerman/Time Life Pictures/Getty Images)

As he became more comfortable in the big league setting, and more confident in his own ability, Aaron's career began to blossom. He hit .314 with 27 homers and 106 RBIs in 1955. In his first three seasons with the Braves, Aaron led the NL in doubles twice, won a batting title, led the league in hits and collected 66 homers, setting the stage for his real coming-out party, the 1957 season.

He led the league in homers for the first time with 44, led the league with 132 RBIs, hit .322, scored 118 runs and led the Braves to the pennant and a World Series matchup with the Yankees. He also won the only MVP award of his career.

It was Aaron's 11th-inning home run that clinched the pennant for the Braves, and he often called that the single most satisfying homer of his career.

Aaron also starred as the Braves upset the heavily favored Yankees and firmly established himself as one of the best players in the game. That, of course, was not news to the National League pitchers, who long since had determined that despite Aaron's casual approach, he meant business when he was standing at the plate.

"He could fall asleep between pitches and still wake up in time to hit the next one," Hall of Fame pitcher Robin Roberts once said of Aaron.

One of the most famous quotes about Aaron has been credited to various sources over the years, but it is believed the person who actually made the comment first was pitcher Curt Simmons, who said of Aaron, "Trying to sneak a fastball past Hank Aaron is like trying to sneak the sunrise past a rooster."

Claude Osteen, another pitcher who was frequently on the losing end of battles against Aaron, once said, "Slapping a rattlesnake across the face with the back of your hand is safer than trying to fool Henry Aaron."

Those, of course, were not the only pitchers Aaron abused over his career. His 755 career homers came against 310 different pitchers. The pitcher he victimized the most often was another Hall of Famer, Don Drysdale, who gave up 17 of Aaron's home run clouts.

Aaron and the Braves again won the NL pennant in 1958, but this time lost the World Series to the Yankees. They tied the Dodgers for the 1959 title and lost in the playoff.

Aaron was just really beginning to show his remarkable ability, however, and one of the most amazing characteristics about Aaron's career was his consistency. From 1955 through 1973, a 19-year run, Aaron hit between 24 and 47 homers every year, drove in 89 or more runs 17 times, and hit .287 or higher 17 times. He had 14 .300 seasons in his career and drove in 100 or more runs 11 times.

He won four home run titles, in 1957, 1963, 1966 and 1967. He topped the 40-homer mark eight times, with his highest total coming when he hit 47 in 1971 at the age of 37.

That season boosted Aaron's career total to 639 homers and left him seriously thinking that he had a chance to break Ruth's record if he continued to stay healthy. He trailed Ruth by 75 homers, and fans and the media were beginning to believe Aaron had a chance at the record and were finally giving him the credit for his success that had been long overdue.

Along with that credit, however, also came racist comments and abuse about a black man challenging the greatest record in sports. Aaron had to put up with death threats and mental abuse for the next two seasons as he pursued the record.

Aaron hit 34 homers in 1972, and added 40 more in 1973 at the age of 39 in just 392 at-bats, but finished the year one shy of tying Ruth, forcing him to go through the entire off season thinking about needing just one homer to tie the record and two to break it.

The Braves opened the 1974 season in Cincinnati, and they wanted Aaron to sit out the series so he could tie and break the record at home. Commissioner Bowie Kuhn, however, ordered that Aaron play in the series, and he didn't take long to make history—homering off Jack Billingham on opening day for his 714th career homer, tying Ruth.

When the Braves got back home to face the Dodgers, on April 8, 1974, Aaron delivered his record-breaking homer, off Al Downing, to pass Ruth. Almost unnoticed was that in the previous at-bat in that game, he had walked and scored, breaking Willie Mays's NL record for runs scored and moving into third place all-time in that category, trailing only Cobb and Ruth.

Aaron wasn't finished, of course, and after completing 1974 with 20 homers, he moved back to Milwaukee to play his final two years in the American

ABOVE: Hank Aaron is congratulated by teammates after breaking Babe Ruth's record of 714 home runs.
(Carl Skalak/Time Life Pictures/Getty Images)

League as the Brewers' designated hitter. He added 22 more homers to his total to finish at 755.

The fact that Aaron was able to persevere and succeed under such intense pressure and scrutiny added even more value to his accomplishments. When he hit his final homer, on July 20, 1976 against California's Dick Drago, his legacy was complete.

Twenty-eight years later, it appears Aaron's record might be under a challenge from Barry Bonds, who began the 2004 season 97 homers behind Aaron. Even if Bonds does eventually catch and pass Aaron's total sometime in the next few seasons, he will not be able

to equal all of Aaron's other accomplishments in the game, on and off the field.

Aaron was a 24-time All-Star in his 23 seasons. He topped the 200-hit mark three times and four more years had 190 or more hits. He led the league in total bases eight times. He scored more than 100 runs 15 times. He definitely proved he was more than a home run hitter.

In his first year of eligibility, Aaron was elected to the Hall of Fame in 1982, receiving 406 of a possible 415 votes.

Ty Cobb

In the movie *Field of Dreams*, Shoeless Joe Jackson's ban from baseball is lifted and he is allowed to once again take the field and play against some of the other legendary figures of the game from the early part of this century.

One player, however, was excluded—Ty Cobb.

"Cobb wanted to come back, but none of us could stand the SOB when he was alive, so we told him to stick it," Jackson said in the movie.

That quote is probably as accurate a portrayal of Cobb as can be made, who unquestionably was one of the greatest hitters and players of his era but made no friends with his aggressive, in-your-face, hell-bent style of play.

No one ever knew for certain what caused Cobb's anger, but many traced it to the shocking murder of his father when Cobb was 18 years old and just beginning his baseball career. The true story was never confirmed, but the elder Cobb was shot and killed by his mother as he climbed through a bedroom window of their Georgia home. Cobb's mother allegedly mistook her husband for a burglar.

There was no doubt that his anger drove Cobb's success in the game and helped him lead the American League in one offensive category or another an astounding 58 times during his 24-year career, which began in 1905 and saw him play all but his final two years with the Detroit Tigers.

"Baseball is not unlike a war," Cobb once said. "And when you get down to it, we batters are the heavy artillery."

In the Rawlings rankings of the game's all-time greatest hitters, Cobb collected 112 points, only three less than the top-ranked hitter of all time, Hank Aaron. In five of the six categories used as the basis for the rankings, Cobb finished second in hits and triples, fourth in doubles and total bases and sixth in RBIs—without finishing in the top 25 in home runs. Despite his low home run total, Cobb still led the AL in slugging percentage eight times.

Most of Cobb's career came in the dead ball era, and he made the most of his ability to slap the ball into the outfield, never stopping as he rounded first base, deciding on the run if the positioning of the outfielder would allow him to stretch the hit into a double.

Born in 1886, Cobb's career began to blossom when a legendary Atlanta sportswriter, Grantland Rice, responded to numerous letters he was receiving about a young phenom playing in Alabama named Cobb by writing a column detailing Cobb's virtues, even though he had never seen Cobb play.

Years later, Rice found out all of those letters had been sent by Cobb himself, using fictitious names.

OPPOSITE: Ty Cobb (left), known as "the Georgia Peach," stands next to another baseball great, "Shoeless Joe" Jackson. (Hulton Archive/Getty Images)

"He could do everything better than any player I ever saw."

—Walter Johnson

That deception might have begun Cobb's notoriety, but he certainly earned the bulk of it by the way he played the game and the results he was able to achieve. He led the AL in batting average 12 times in a 13-year span, beginning when he hit .350 in 1907 at the age of 20. Over the next 13 seasons, the only time he failed to win the batting title was in 1916—when he hit .371. Three times he topped the .400 mark.

The left-handed-hitting Cobb had 10 200-hit seasons and led the league in hits eight times. In 23 of his 24 seasons, his average topped .300, and his career average of .367 still ranks as the best of all time. When he was 39 years old, he went six for six in one game, including hitting three homers.

What kept Cobb from getting more respect and earning even more praise as the game's greatest player—until he was overshadowed by the slugging of Babe Ruth—was his penchant for getting in trouble and his battles with opposing players, his own teammates, and fans.

One time in the minor leagues he got into a fight with his roommate because Cobb was mad the roommate had taken a bath before he did. Cobb did not want to be second in anything.

On other occasions Cobb flung his bat at pitcher Carl Mays and went into the stands to go after a heckling fan. He often played under police protection when the Tigers were on the road.

Despite all of the allegations that Cobb intentionally spiked opponents when he was sliding into bases, Cobb maintained that he did so only twice, and that both were deserved. Still, the fear of being spiked often made opponents move quicker to get out of Cobb's way.

"When he was in his prime, he had half the AL scared stiff," said Detroit manager Hugh Jennings.

Cobb, who had an unorthodox style of gripping the bat with his hands apart, was an intense student of the game. Batting against Walter Johnson, he crowded the plate more than normal, knowing it would force Johnson to pitch outside. When Johnson fell behind in the count and had to come back with an inside pitch, Cobb was ready to crush it.

Even though opponents didn't care for Cobb, they had to give him credit for his ability.

"He could do everything better than any player I ever saw," Johnson said.

When he retired in 1928 at the age of 42, Cobb owned 90 major league records. What always bothered him intensely, however, was that he never played on a World Series championship team. His Tigers won three AL pennants, but each time lost the World Series.

Even after he was retired, Cobb's style of play never changed. In an old-timers' game at Yankee Stadium when he was 60 years old, Cobb told the catcher to move back because he was afraid the bat would slip out of his hands and hit the catcher.

As soon as the catcher complied with his request, Cobb laid down a bunt and beat it out for a hit.

OPPOSITE: Ty Cobb at bat in this June 28, 1928 photo. (AP/WWP)

No. 3

Stan Musial

Stan Musial never said he was worried or upset about going zero for four during a game. The way he figured it, it meant he would get three or four hits the next day.

For many hitters in the major leagues, that would be wishful thinking. For Musial, it was simply a matter of reality. Because Ted Williams played in Boston and Joe DiMaggio played in New York, the universal opinion in the late 1940s and 1950s was that they were the two best players in the game. The player many observers were forgetting, however, was a member of the St. Louis Cardinals, and at least according to the Rawlings rankings, he was the best of the three.

Musial finished in third place on the Rawlings scale of the game's greatest hitters of all time with 99 points. He was the only hitter to rank in the top 25 in all six categories that were the basis of the rankings—home runs, hits, RBIs, doubles, triples and total bases. Musial is tied for 23rd all-time in career homers, ranks fourth in career hits, is fifth in career RBIs, is third in career doubles, is tied for 19th in career triples and is second all-time in career total bases.

Musial won the universal respect of his teammates, opponents, media and fans during his 22-year career as a member of the Cardinals. He made his major league debut in September 1941, missed the 1945 season to serve in the navy and retired after the 1963 season.

The left-handed hitter with a unique batting stance that some observers said looked like he was peeking around a corner won seven batting titles between 1943 and 1957. He was named the National League's MVP three times, in 1943, 1946 and 1948, and finished second four other times.

Musial finished his career with an average of .331 and the remarkable accomplishment of having the exact same number of hits, 1,815, at home and on the road, getting two hits in his final career game in order to be able to make that claim.

It was playing against the Dodgers in Brooklyn that he earned his famous nickname, when a fan, knowing how much Musial had abused Dodger pitching over the years, saw him walking up to the plate and lamented, "Here comes that man again." From then on, he was known as Stan "the Man" Musial.

Brooklyn's Preacher Roe might have had the best strategy of any pitcher in the league when he was asked once how he tried to pitch to Musial.

"I throw him four wide ones, and then I try to pick him off," Roe said.

Another player who had more than his share of success in his career, Ty Cobb, never faced Musial but saw him play enough to come away impressed with

OPPOSITE: Cardinals great Stan Musial. (Bob Gomel/Time Life Pictures/Getty Images)

"No man has ever been a perfect ballplayer. Stan Musial, however, is the **closest thing to perfection** in the game today. He's certainly one of the great hitters of all time."

—Ty Cobb

his abilities and secure in his knowledge that Musial was one of the game's greats.

"No man has ever been a perfect ballplayer," Cobb once said. "Stan Musial, however, is the closest thing to perfection in the game today. He's certainly one of the great hitters of all time."

Musial was blessed with extraordinary ability to play baseball as a young boy growing up in Donora, Pennsylvania. He signed with the Cardinals after pleading with his father, who wanted his son to go to college.

It appeared a couple of years later that Musial's career was over before it really had begun. He was primarily a left-handed pitcher in the Cardinals' minor league system, but was playing some games in the outfield and was there one day when he fell trying to catch a ball and landed hard on his shoulder. His manager, Dickie Kerr, wouldn't let Musial quit and instead converted him into a full-time outfielder.

A year later, Musial had rocketed through the farm system and was beginning his Hall of Fame career with the Cardinals.

"I could always hit," Musial once said. "It is not something I ever had to think too much about. A lot of guys are very scientific about it. It just seemed to come naturally, even when I was growing up."

Musial said the key to him was not trying to be overly analytical or trying to do too much when he went up to the plate.

"The secret of hitting is physical relaxation, mental concentration, and don't hit the fly ball to center," he said.

Musial hit .300 every season until he was 38 years old and then at age 41 came back to hit .330. He drove in 100 or more runs 10 times, and even though he never hit 40 home runs in a season, he would have won the Triple Crown in 1948 had he not had one home run come in a game that later was rained out, preventing him from tying Ralph Kiner for the league lead in homers.

He played in 24 All-Star games, hitting six homers. He led the NL in doubles eight times; in hits, on-base percentage and slugging percentage six times; and in runs and triples five times.

When Musial reached the 3,000-hit plateau in 1958, he was only the eighth player to join that club and was the first since Paul Waner recorded his 3,000[th] hit in 1925. When Musial retired, he was the NL career leader in hits, doubles, RBIs and total bases.

Of all of his places among the top 25 career players, the spot Musial appears to be in the greatest jeopardy of losing in the coming years is in home runs. His total of 475, which ties him for 23rd all-time, could well be fewer homers than Juan Gonzalez (now at 429), Jeff Bagwell (419) or Frank Thomas (418) hit when their careers are finished.

OPPOSITE: Stan Musial set to swat another pitch out of the park. (John G. Zimmerman/Time Life Pictures/Getty Images)

No. 4
Tris Speaker

When the Boston Red Sox could not pay both their hotel bill and their rent of the stadium they used in Little Rock, Arkansas, for spring training in 1908, they reached an agreement with the owner of the local minor league team.

The Red Sox paid what cash they had to the hotel, and they left two ballplayers behind as payment for their stadium rent. It didn't take long to realize they had overpaid.

One of the players was outfielder Tris Speaker, who played well enough in his short stay in Arkansas that the Red Sox quickly bought him back for $500 before the owner of the Little Rock club could sell him to another team.

Speaker went on to become a star with the Red Sox and in the American League, but the biggest problem he faced was that he had the bad misfortune to come along in the same era as the Tigers' Ty Cobb, who always seemed to overshadow Speaker's accomplishments.

Four times in his 22-year career Speaker hit .380 or better, but he only managed to defeat Cobb once for the AL batting title, in 1916.

Speaker was a similar hitter to Cobb, collecting far more doubles and triples than home runs, and it was no surprise that when Speaker retired he was second all-time to Cobb in career hits. He remained in second place until 1962, when he was finally passed by Stan Musial.

Musial and Cobb were two of the only three players who topped Speaker's total of 79 points in the Rawlings scale ranking the greatest hitters of all time. Despite not ranking in the top 25 all-time in home runs or RBIs, Speaker's point total was accumulated by his all-time lead in doubles, ranking fifth in hits, sixth in triples and 13th in total bases. Speaker's doubles total of 792 has remained as the record since his retirement in 1929, 68 more than Cobb, who ranks fourth all-time.

There was one other area where Speaker did surpass Cobb—he was a key component on three world championship teams, with the Red Sox in 1912 and 1915 and as the player-manager with the Indians in 1920.

Born in 1888, Speaker fell off a horse when he was a young boy and broke his right arm. That forced him to begin using his left arm as his dominant arm, and he quickly became a pitcher. It wasn't long, however, before he shifted to the outfield because of his hitting ability.

Speaker was playing minor league ball in Houston in 1907 when his contract was sold to the Red Sox 30 minutes before a scout from the St. Louis Browns arrived ready to make an offer to purchase Speaker's contract.

OPPOSITE: Boston Red Sox outfielder Tris Speaker, shown here in a 1912 photo. (AP/WWP)

"The American boy starts swinging the bat about as soon as he can lift one."

—Tris Speaker

Speaker developed into a star in Boston and was there when Babe Ruth broke in with the Red Sox in 1914 and 1915. Despite winning the World Series that year, Boston President Joe Lannon tried to cut Speaker's salary—which had been the highest in baseball—from $15,000 to $9,000 in 1916, based on the fact that Speaker's batting average had declined for four consecutive seasons. Speaker also had received a lot of small perks in his contract over the years, earning an extra $50 every time he hit the Bull Durham sign at the Red Sox' park, first at Huntington Avenue and later Fenway Park.

When Speaker rejected the contract offer, he did not report to spring training until he got word that everything would be worked out. Speaker believed that meant he would receive his asking price of $16,000 a season, but quickly found out it meant something else—his contract was sold to Cleveland for $50,000.

Speaker continued to enjoy success with the Indians, although he again was playing in Cobb's, and now Ruth's, shadow.

Speaker was involved in a situation that, had it been resolved differently, might have changed the course of history. In 1918, the Indians were challenging the Red Sox for the AL pennant. On August 28, Speaker got into an argument with umpire Tom Connolly during a game in Philadelphia. The argument was viewed as an assault on the umpire, and Speaker was suspended for the rest of the season.

The Red Sox went on to win the pennant by 2 1/2 games over the Indians. If Speaker had not been suspended for the final month of the season, Cleveland might have won—and 1918 might not be remembered throughout New England as the last year the Red Sox won the World Series.

Much of Speaker's reputation throughout baseball was earned by his defensive ability in center field, which again overshadowed how truly gifted he was as an offensive player.

Between 1912 and 1925, Speaker failed to win the batting title despite hitting .383 in 1912, .363 in 1913, .388 in 1920, .378 in 1922, .380 in 1923 and .389 in 1925. During the 1912 season, Speaker had three separate hitting streaks of 20 games or more.

Over a 15-year period, Speaker averaged .356 with 42 doubles, 12 triples and six homers, like Cobb playing the bulk of his career during the dead ball era. Nicknamed The Gray Eagle because of his prematurely gray hair, Speaker stood deep in the batter's box and held his bad hip high as he attacked the ball from his closed, crouching stance.

Speaker always attributed his success to God-given ability and the fact that he had fallen in love with baseball at an early age.

"The American boy starts swinging the bat about as soon as he can lift one," he once said.

OPPOSITE: Baseball legends Ty Cobb, left, and Tris Speaker, teammates with the Philadelphia Athletics, pose in the dugout for this September 9, 1928 photo. (AP/WWP)

No. 5
Willie Mays

There is no question that Willie Mays ranks among the greatest hitters in the history of baseball, but like Ted Williams, his ranking could have been even higher if he had not missed almost two years of his career serving in the military.

Mays was coming off his National League Rookie of the Year campaign with the New York Giants in 1951 when he got word he had been drafted into the army. As a 20-year-old rookie in 1951, Mays hit .274 with 20 homers and 68 RBIs in 121 games after being recalled from the minors in May.

He played in only 34 games in 1952, then missed the rest of that season and all of 1953. If he had not missed that time, Mays certainly would have had a chance to break Babe Ruth's then-career record of 714 homers and would have moved up in other categories as well.

Despite missing that time, Mays still emerged as the fifth best hitter of all time on the Rawlings' scale. He collected 78 points on the strength of ranking third all time in career homers with 660, 11th all time in career hits, ninth all time in career RBIs, and third all-time in total bases.

In addition to missing those two seasons while he was in the military, Mays's power numbers also were hurt by the Giants' move to San Francisco from New York after the 1957 season. Candlestick Park proved to be a much tougher park to hit home runs than the Polo Grounds had been.

The Giants signed the 5-foot-11, 180-pound Mays the day he graduated from high school in Birmingham, Alabama, three years after he had begun playing with the Black Barons of the Negro Leagues. In his first season, Mays's father, a semipro player who worked in a steel mill, allowed Willie to play only home games so he would remain in school.

The right-handed-hitting Mays spent just one year and a month in the minors, being recalled from Minneapolis when he was hitting a lofty .477. Still, he had doubts he was ready for the majors and began his career with an 0-for-12 streak that left him crying in the clubhouse.

Manager Leo Durocher came up to Mays and put his arm around his shoulders and told him, "I don't care if you never get a hit; you're my center fielder."

That reassurance helped Mays, who got his first career hit the following day—a towering home run off Hall of Famer Warren Spahn that cleared the left field roof at the Polo Grounds.

Another 0-for-12 streak followed, however, before Mays finally settled down and began playing the game the way he had always played—with a smile on his face and an intense desire to succeed. It was not unusual for Mays to play a doubleheader at the Polo Grounds and then be found playing stickball with the kids in Harlem.

OPPOSITE: Willie Mays slams one high and away. (John G. Zimmerman/Time Life Pictures/Getty Images)

"My idea was to do everything better than anybody else ever had. I concentrated on every aspect of the game."

—Willie Mays

His consistency was one of Mays's greatest strengths. He played in a record-tying 24 All-Star games and had a career average of .302 to go with his 660 homers. He played in 150 or more games for 13 consecutive years, the first seven years of that stretch coming when teams played only 154 games. He drove in 100 or more runs 10 times and scored 100 or more runs for 12 consecutive years. For 11 years he hit 35 or more homers, twice topping 50 homers and four more times hitting more than 40. He recorded 300 or more total bases for 13 consecutive years.

Mays won the NL batting title in 1954 and led the league in homers four times. He led in stolen bases four consecutive years and also led the league in triples three times, becoming one of the first hitters in the history of the game to combine speed and power. He was the first player ever to hit 50 or more homers and steal 20 or more bases in the same season. Unlike a typical power hitter, Mays never struck out more than 100 times in a season until his 21st year in the majors, when he was 40 years old.

Mays was a two-time MVP, in 1954 and 1965, and led the Giants to four pennants and trips to the World Series.

He is even the answer to an often-asked trivia question. He was the hitter who was on deck when teammate Bobby Thomson hit the famous home run off Ralph Branca in the 1951 playoff game against the Dodgers that won the pennant for the Giants, capping their rally from a 13 1/2-game deficit.

"My idea was to do everything better than anybody else ever had," Mays once said. "I concentrated on every aspect of the game."

To hear his managers and opponents talk, Mays came incredibly close to reaching that goal.

"If somebody came up and hit .450, stole 100 bases and performed a miracle on the field every day, I'd still look you in the eye and say Willie was better," Durocher once said.

Charlie Fox, Mays's manager later in his career, added, "The man dominated a game like no other player in the history of the game. I don't think there was any play he couldn't make."

Opposing manager Gene Mauch was quoted as saying about Mays, "He was the greatest ballplayer I ever saw in most departments. I don't know how many people have driven in 150 runs in a year, hit 50 home runs in a year, batted .350 in a year, stolen 50 bases in a year and played his position peerlessly."

Mauch exaggerated only slightly—Mays's top RBI year was 141, his top stolen base year was 40, and his top average was .347.

Mays returned to New York to spend his final two seasons with the Mets in 1972 and 1973. He was elected to the Hall of Fame in 1979.

OPPOSITE: One of the most consistent players to ever pick up a bat, Willie Mays blasts yet another home run. (Bob Gomel/Time Life Pictures/Getty Images)

No. 6

Honus Wagner

The son of a coal miner from Pennsylvania, Honus Wagner was able to use baseball as an escape from a life in the mines. He already was working loading coal cars when he was 12 years old, earning 79 cents a ton. Wagner usually was able to load two tons a day.

That hard work made him appreciate the game he loved, and he often walked a dozen miles to climb a tree and watch the Pittsburgh Pirates play.

Wagner, who also spent some time working in a brother's barber shop while he was a teenager, got his chance to play baseball when he was spotted by scout Edward G. Barrow, a legendary baseball man who spent 25 years building the Yankees' dynasty. Barrow had gone to Ohio to watch Wagner's older brother, Al, but saw Wagner throwing rocks and signed him on the spot. His first baseball contract was for $35 a month.

Wagner wasn't worried about money—he just wanted to play. He broke into the majors as an outfielder, and he didn't settle in as a shortstop until his sixth season, when he was 29 years old, but today is still regarded by many baseball historians as the greatest shortstop who ever played.

He also was a pretty fair hitter. On the Rawlings scale of the greatest hitters of all time, Wagner finished sixth with a total of 74 points. He ranks eighth all-time in hits, third in triples, 17th in RBIs, eighth in doubles and 20th in total bases.

Wagner was born in 1874 and was old by baseball standards at the time he made his major league debut in 1897 at the age of 23. He was already a quality player, however, and was remarkably consistent over his entire 21-year career.

A right-handed hitter who kept his hands apart when he batted and specialized in hitting line drives to all fields, Wagner earned his nickname, "The Flying Dutchman," because of his fearless style of running the bases. It was not unusual for opposing players to simply move out of his way so Wagner would not run them over.

Wagner posted a .300 or better average for 17 consecutive seasons and won eight National League batting titles, including four in a row between 1906 and 1909. His average did not fall below .300 for a season until he was 40 years old. Wagner also led the league in slugging percentage six times and drove in 100 or more runs nine times. He led the league in doubles seven times, in triples three times and in RBIs five times. Wagner finished with a lifetime average of .329, and when he retired he was the National League career leader in hits, runs, doubles, triples and singles. He also stole 722 bases.

Wagner led the Pirates to four National League pennants during his career, and during his famous showdown with Ty Cobb's Tigers in the 1909 World

OPPOSITE: Baseball great Honus Wagner smashes one deep and away. (Photo courtesy of the Pittsburgh Pirates)

> ## "Babe Ruth was the game's greatest personality and its greatest home run hitter. Ty Cobb was the greatest of all hitters—but there is no question that Wagner was the greatest all-around ballplayer who ever lived."
>
> —Edward G. Barrow

Series, he outplayed Cobb and helped the Pirates win the world championship. A frustrated Cobb said afterward, "That damn Dutchman is the only man in the game I can't scare."

Unlike Cobb, Wagner made no efforts to promote himself or discuss his own abilities, preferring to let his performance speak for itself. Some of his contemporaries, however, considered him the equal of Cobb and Babe Ruth if not a better overall player.

Legendary manager John McGraw considered Wagner the greatest player in the history of the game, ahead of Ruth and Cobb. Part of that opinion might have been a National League bias, but McGraw also put an emphasis on the fact that Wagner was a shortstop and was putting up some monstrous offensive numbers, while Cobb and Ruth were outfielders.

"Babe Ruth was the game's greatest personality and its greatest home run hitter," Barrow once said. "Ty Cobb was the greatest of all hitters—but there is no question that Wagner was the greatest all-around ballplayer who ever lived."

Legendary pitcher Walter Johnson agreed, and he only had to face Wagner a few times since they were in opposite leagues.

"There wasn't anything he couldn't do—hit, run and field," Johnson said. "I'm glad he stayed on his side of the fence [in the NL]."

When the Baseball Hall of Fame inducted its first members in 1936, Wagner was one of the five original inductees along with Cobb, Ruth, Johnson and Christy Mathewson.

Like all great players, Wagner had a flare for the dramatic, like when he stood up to challenge Cobb and the Tigers. Another moment came in 1915, when he hit one of his few home runs to break up a no-hit bid by Grover Cleveland Alexander in the eighth inning, the only hit Alexander allowed in the game.

Wagner was not as famous as the other great players in the American League, like Cobb, but he was loyal, turning down offers to jump to the American League for a higher salary, saying he preferred to stay in Pittsburgh.

Wagner also was a man of convictions, and his stance against promoting cigarettes has created the most famous baseball card of all time. Wagner's card, T-206, was produced in 1909 by a tobacco company, and when Wagner found out the company was using the card to promote the sale of cigarettes, he asked that the card be destroyed. Only a few cards remained in circulation, and today that card is considered the most valuable card on the market.

OPPOSITE: Honus Wagner's T-206 baseball card—arguably the most famous baseball card in history. (Chris Hondros/Getty Images)

WAGNER, PITTSBURG

No. 7
Carl Yastrzemski

Fans of the Boston Red Sox were worried at the beginning of the 1961 season because their star player, Ted Williams, had retired at the end of the previous year and now the team was turning to a 22-year-old rookie to replace Williams in left field.

When that rookie struggled in the early part of the season, hitting .220 through May, the fans went beyond worried. What they didn't know, however, was that all of that worry was definitely misplaced.

That rookie, Carl Yastrzemski, went on to not only become a star but to actually surpass many of Williams's career accomplishments, not only with the Red Sox but among the game's all-time greats.

On the Rawlings scale, Yastrzemski came in as the seventh best hitter of all time, totaling 73 points. He ranks sixth all-time in career hits, 11th all-time in career RBI, seventh all-time in career doubles and seventh all-time in total bases.

It took the Boston fans some time to accept Yastrzemski, but that put him in good company. Williams always had a love-hate relationship with the Red Sox' faithful and media during his long career, and Yastrzemski also found the fans often wanting more than he gave them—except during the final month of the 1967 season.

Yastrzemski had won his first of three American League batting titles in 1963 and was closing in on another crown in 1967. More importantly, however, the Red Sox were battling for their first pennant in 21 years and Yastrzemski was threatening to win the Triple Crown.

The race came down to the final two days of the season. The Red Sox were playing the Minnesota Twins at Fenway and had to win both games, while the Tigers had to lose to the Angels for Boston to win the pennant.

Going into those last two days, Yastrzemski was leading the batting race and the RBI title, but found himself tied with the Twins' Harmon Killebrew for the home run title with 43 each.

In the next to last game of the season, Yastrzemski homered and the Red Sox won, but Killebrew homered too, and they were still tied. Both the pennant race and the individual battle went down to the season's final day.

After having trouble sleeping, all Yasztremski did was go four for four, including delivering a key two-run single which tied the game, and lead the Red Sox to the win. When Detroit lost, the Impossible Dream, as the season was called, had been completed.

Yastrzemski also won the Triple Crown, winning the batting title with a .326 mark to go along with his 121 RBIs and his 44 homers, sharing that title with Killebrew. He still is the last major leaguer to win the Triple Crown.

OPPOSITE: Boston Red Sox outfielder Carl Yastrzemski poses in this 1967 photo. (AP/WWP)

> ## "Carl does everything there is to do in the game exceptionally well. He is **the best player in the league**, and he would be the best at some other position if he played there."
>
> —Dick Williams

He followed up his strong finish to the regular season by hitting .400 with three homers in the World Series, but saw his Red Sox lose the Series to the Cardinals in seven games.

Yastrzemski proved that he was at his best in the clutch. In the final 39 games of the season, he hit .379 with nine homers and 22 RBIs. He was an easy choice as the league's MVP.

The third batting championship of Yastrzemski's career came the following year, when he led the league hitting just .301, the lowest mark ever by a batting champion. In the year of the pitcher, however, the league average was just .230.

Yastrzemski also led the Red Sox to the 1975 American League pennant, only to lose the World Series again, this time to the Reds. He also was on the 1978 team which lost the AL East title in a playoff game to the Yankees.

Like Williams a left-handed hitter, Yastrzemski won praise for how hard he worked to make himself the best hitter he could be. He spent hours in the batting cage and studying the game.

In the 30 biggest games of his career, the final 12 games of the 1967 season, the 17 postseason games and the 1978 playoff game, Yastrzemski combined to hit .430 with 10 homers, 29 RBIs and 31 runs scored.

The son of a potato farmer, Yastrzemski signed with the Red Sox as a shortstop after playing one year at Notre Dame. Converted to an outfielder during his two years in the minors, Yastrzemski went on to play 23 years with the Red Sox, matching the major league record for the longest tenure with one team. He shares the mark with Baltimore's Brooks Robinson.

Yastrzemski became the first American League hitter to collect 3,000 career hits with 400 or more homers. He hit 40 or more homers twice and twice led the league in slugging percentage. He also led the league in doubles three times. One indication of the respect he received was that he was intentionally walked 190 times in his career, a record at the time of his retirement since those records were first kept in 1955.

When he retired following the 1983 season, Yastrzemski had played in 18 All-Star games and was the franchise's career leader in eight major offensive categories—games, at-bats, runs, hits, doubles, total bases, RBIs, and extra-base hits. During his career, he led the AL in 23 offensive categories.

Even though he finished with a career .285 average to go with his 452 lifetime homers, Yastrzemski topped the .300 mark six times. He was elected to the Hall of Fame in 1989.

"Carl does everything there is to do in the game exceptionally well," said Dick Williams, his manager, in 1969. "He is the best player in the league, and he would be the best at some other position if he played there."

ABOVE: Carl Yastrzemski follows through on his 3000th hit during the eighth inning against the New York Yankees on September 11, 1979. (AP/WWP)

No. 8 (Tie)

Pete Rose

The debate over whether Pete Rose should be reinstated to baseball and made eligible for election to the Hall of Fame is one that will linger for some time. What is not in doubt, however, is that when he played, Rose was one of the greatest hitters the game has known.

Rose's place among baseball's greats has been tarnished in recent years because of his reluctant admittance after 14 years of denial that he did bet on baseball when he was the manager of the Cincinnati Reds.

The Rawlings rankings of the game's greatest hitters, however, is able to overlook that controversy because it deals strictly with the statistical data accumulated by a player during his career. Rose's numbers speak for themself.

He is the all-time hits leader in baseball history with 4,256. He ranks second all-time in career doubles. Despite being primarily a singles and doubles hitter, he ranks sixth all-time in career total bases. Those three finishes earned Rose 69 points on the Rawlings scale, leaving him in a tie as the eighth best hitter of all time with Babe Ruth.

What is most impressive about Rose's career is that he was not blessed with God-given ability or unnatural physical powers. He was able to get a tryout with his hometown Cincinnati Reds through his uncle, who was a scout. When he joined the major league team in spring training of 1963, he was not projected as a star or even a major leaguer for that matter.

It was during a game that spring when Yankees pitcher Whitey Ford reportedly noticed Rose's all-out hustle and gave him the nickname which remained throughout his career—Charlie Hustle. If there was one attribute which really made Rose into a top-caliber player, it was his hustle—sprinting to first base on a walk, stretching a single into a double, diving head first into a base, knocking over the catcher if that was the only way he would be able to score. He once hit 30 triples in a minor league season.

"Rose is a self-made person," his longtime manager with the Reds, Sparky Anderson, once said. "No one jumped out of their shoes to sign him when he got out of high school. He made himself into what he is, and to do that you've got to be a competitor."

Rose was voted the NL Rookie of the Year in 1963 despite hitting only .273. His average fell to .269 in his second season, hardly a proper indication of the career that was to blossom in his third year.

Rose kept working on his hitting, studying the pitchers, and figuring out the adjustments he had to make to be successful. In 1965 he led the NL with 209 hits and hit .312—the first of nine consecutive seasons in which he topped that plateau. Following one off year, he hit .300 or better again for five more

OPPOSITE: Cincinnati Reds third baseman Pete Rose removes his helmet for the crowd after his record-breaking 4193rd career hit on September 11, 1985. (Hulton Archive/Getty Images)

"Hitting is such a challenge. Realistically, it is probably the hardest thing to do in any sport. Think about it. You've got a round ball, a round bat, and the object is to hit it square."

—Pete Rose

consecutive years, a total of 15 .300-plus seasons in 17 years. He hit .300 for the final time in 1981 at the age of .40

A switch hitter, Rose led the league in hits seven times and enjoyed 10 200-plus hit seasons. He won three batting titles, and the way he won two of them again displayed his competitiveness along with his other skills.

In 1968, Rose needed to go six for nine in the final two games of the season to defeat Matty Alou of the Pirates and win the batting crown with a .335 mark. Alou finished at .332. The next year, the race again came down to the final day, this time Rose battling it out with the Pirates' Roberto Clemente. Rose beat out a bunt in his final at-bat of the season and won the title with a .348 average. Clemente hit .345.

Also the career leader in games played with 3,562, Rose was the NL's MVP in 1973 and played on three world championship teams (the 1975 and 1976 Reds and the 1980 Philadelphia Phillies) and in six World Series. An 18-time All-Star, Rose also mounted the last serious challenge to Joe DiMaggio's 56-game hitting streak when he hit in 44 consecutive games in 1978.

He led the NL in doubles five times, and from 1965 through 1979, he averaged 204 hits a season. For the best 15-year period of their careers, Ty Cobb averaged 194 hits a year and Stan Musial averaged 197 hits.

Rose forever earned his place in baseball's history books, if not in the Hall of Fame, on September 11, 1985, when he collected the 4,193rd hit of his career, a single off the Padres' Eric Show, to break Cobb's all-time hits record. Rose was 44 at the time, and it was one of more than 1,000 career hits Rose accumulated after his 38th birthday.

Rose also played in an era when the National League pitching was particularly tough. At least nine NL pitchers from the 1960s and 1970s already have been elected to the Hall of Fame.

Rose was proud of his accomplishment, and deservedly so. As much as some critics might say his attitude is cocky and arrogant, Rose's supporters can say he earned the right to boast about what he had achieved.

"Hitting is such a challenge," Rose once said. "Realistically, it is probably the hardest thing to do in any sport. Think about it. You've got a round ball, a round bat, and the object is to hit it square."

Whether or not he is ever accepted into Cooperstown, Rose will have the internal satisfaction of knowing he succeeded at that challenge more than anybody else in history.

ABOVE: Pete Rose slashes his record-breaking hit to left center field against the San Diego Padres. (Getty Images)

No. 8 (Tie)

Babe Ruth

During the 1920s, there is no doubt that Babe Ruth was the most dominating force in professional sports and that he had earned a status in America that went even beyond sports.

Whether he really did save the game of baseball or not following the 1919 Black Sox scandal, there can be no debate that Ruth came along at a time when baseball needed a star and positive press, and he quickly became a legend as fans flocked to the park to watch his power display. He changed the way the game was played, emphasizing the power of the home run, and was able to bring fans back to the ballpark in hopes of seeing him hit a home run.

Ruth was raised in a Baltimore orphanage, turned over to the priests by his parents because they were having a hard time raising him. It was at the orphanage that Ruth learned baseball, and when he was 19 he signed a contract with the Baltimore club of the International League. The following year he was sold to the Red Sox after hitting only one career homer in the minor leagues.

Ruth came to the major leagues as a pitcher, and if he had not been such a prodigious hitter, he might well be in the Hall of Fame today as one of the game's greatest left-handed pitchers. He won 23 games for the Red Sox in 1916 and 24 games in 1917, and he held the record for most consecutive scoreless innings in the World Series until Whitey Ford broke that mark in the 1960s.

By 1918, the Red Sox realized how Ruth could help them with more than his pitching ability, and he began to play the outfield in between his pitching assignments. By the following year, 1919, he had become a full-time outfielder and broke the then-major league record for home runs in a season with 29.

It was the first of three consecutive seasons in which Ruth broke that record, although to the Red Sox' everlasting shame, the final two records came with Ruth wearing a New York Yankees' uniform.

Ruth was sold to the Yankees before the 1920 season for $125,000, a move that has never been forgotten by Red Sox fans over the years. The Red Sox, of course, have never won a World Series since 1918.

Many baseball historians consider Ruth the greatest player the game has ever known, but on the Rawlings scale of selecting the game's greatest hitters, Ruth came in tied for eighth with Pete Rose with 69 points. He ranks second all-time in home runs, second in RBIs and fifth in total bases.

There is a tendency to associate Ruth only with home runs, and while that is understandable, it definitely isn't true. He had a lifetime average of .342 and in 1923, the year Yankee Stadium opened, hit .393. Of course he also homered in the first game played in

OPPOSITE: Boxing great Jack Dempsey presents New York Yankees slugger Babe Ruth with a king-sized bat before a game between the Red Sox and the Yankees. (AP/WWP)

the new ballpark. During his 22-year career, he hit .370 or better six times.

Ruth is best known for hitting 60 homers in 1927, but many historians believe his 1921 season was the greatest single season a baseball player has ever produced. That year he hit 59 homers, drove in 171 runs, scored 177 runs, walked 144 times, hit 44 doubles, had 16 triples and batted .378.

Twice, Ruth hit more home runs individually than every other team in the American League hit as a team. In 1920, Ruth hit 54 homers, and the next closest team to the Yankees was the St. Louis Browns, who combined to hit 50 homers. In 1927, the year he hit 60, the Philadelphia Athletics had the second highest team total in the league with 56.

Ruth, who used a bat that weighed a whopping 54 ounces—about 20 ounces more than most modern-day hitters—topped 50 or more home runs four times and 10 times topped the 40-homer mark. He led the league in homers 12 times and topped the AL in RBIs five times. He had a remarkable lifetime slugging percentage of .690. Between 1926 and 1933, his offensive success also was affected by the fact that he led the league in walks seven times in an eight-year span, despite the fact that Lou Gehrig batted behind him.

As important as his individual success was, Ruth's performance helped make the Yankees the most dominant team in baseball. His New York teams won four world championships and seven pennants during Ruth's career. Ruth aided those championships by hitting 15 additional homers in the World Series.

One of those homers is perhaps the most controversial of Ruth's career. The debate still rages about whether Ruth was "calling his shot" when he pointed to the center field stands just before hitting a long homer off the Cubs' Charlie Root in the third game of the 1932 Series.

There is no debate that Ruth made a gesture with his raised hand, but many who were there that day insist that Ruth was not pointing to center field but merely indicating that he had one strike left. The legend has grown, however, that Ruth was indicating he was going to hit the next pitch for a home run, which was exactly what he did.

Ruth played his final season with the Boston Braves in 1935, retiring shortly after he hit three home runs in a game at Forbes Field at the age of 40.

Those homers increased his lifetime total to 714 and earned him a little more notice than his first homer had produced, on May 6, 1915, the day before the headlines of the time were dominated by the sinking of the Lusitania by a German submarine.

OPPOSITE: Babe Ruth clouts a towering home run. (AP/WWP)

No. 10
Eddie Murray

In his speech when he was inducted into the Hall of Fame in 2003, Eddie Murray borrowed an idea from Ted Williams. Never a favorite of the media, Murray said he must have been a pretty good player or he never would have been elected in his first year of eligibility.

As had been the case with Williams, the writers really had no choice but to vote for Murray despite their personal feelings toward him. It is hard to ignore someone who averaged 25 homers and 95 RBIs for a 20-year period during a 21-year career. Murray also earned his place in the Hall when he became only the third hitter in history to reach both the 3,000-hit mark and become a member of the 500-home run club, following Hank Aaron and Willie Mays.

On the Rawlings scale of the game's greatest hitters, Murray finished in 10th place with 66 points. He ranks 19th all-time in career home runs, 12th all-time in career hits, eighth all-time in career RBIs, 17th all-time in career doubles and eighth all-time in career total bases.

While Stan Musial was the only hitter to place in the top 25 all-time in all of the six categories used to compile the Rawlings rankings, Murray was one of only three players—along with Aaron and Ty Cobb—to rank in the top 25 in five of the six categories, missing out only in triples.

Murray might just also be the best switch hitter of all time, ranking as the all-time leader in RBIs among switch hitters and as the runner-up in home runs to Mickey Mantle.

"He was as prepared a hitter as I've ever seen," said Mike Hargrove, Murray's opponent as a player and later his manager with the Cleveland Indians. "He studied what the pitcher did to hitters ahead of him and what they did to hitters comparable to him. He wasn't always right, but he was right more often than other people were."

Murray's trademark, other than the difficulties he had with the media, was his consistency. For much of his career, he was a teammate of Cal Ripken's with the Baltimore Orioles, and they definitely developed a good Oriole-bad Oriole following among fans as well as reporters. The fact remains, however, that Murray was almost as consistent as Ripken.

When Ripken was breaking Lou Gehrig's record for consecutive games played, Murray was playing in 150 or more games for 16 seasons, including a streak of 444 consecutive games. He hit 20 or more homers in 16 seasons, although he never hit 40 in a year—the only member of the 500-home run club never to top that mark. He also drove in at least 75 runs in a season for 20 consecutive years, a major league record.

Murray also was at his best in the clutch. In 238 career at-bats with the bases loaded during his career

OPPOSITE: Eddie Murray flawlessly executes a hit during a game at Camden Yards. (Doug Pensinger/Getty Images)

"He had a presence about him when he came to the plate. He was strong and quick, one of those guys who's a great athlete. He was not just a one-dimensional guy who was strong or who could make contact. He could do both—often."

—Former White Sox pitcher Britt Burns

with the Orioles, Dodgers, Mets and Indians, he posted a .399 average with 19 homers, 298 RBIs, 22 walks and a .739 slugging percentage. His 19 career grand slams is second all-time to Gehrig's 23. Sparky Anderson once walked Murray intentionally with the bases loaded and did not apologize for it.

"Other people may disagree, but if you're asking me what player I'd want up there to win a game, for me it's Eddie Murray," Anderson once said.

Murray, who was one of 10 children, saw three of his brothers play in the minor leagues and brother Rich make the major leagues with the Giants. He also was a teammate of Hall of Famer Ozzie Smith at Locke High School in Los Angeles.

An eight-time All-Star, Murray was the AL Rookie of the Year with the Orioles in 1977 when he hit .283 with 27 homers and 88 RBIs. He led the Orioles to the 1979 pennant and to the world championship in 1983, when he hit two homers in the clinching Game 5 of the Series against the Phillies.

Multiple-homer games were nothing new for Murray. He holds the major league record by hitting home runs from both sides of the plate in 11 different games in his career. He also had three three-homer games.

The only year Murray led the league in homers or RBIs, however, was the strike year of 1981. He did drive in 100 or more runs six times, including in four consecutive years.

"He could do things with the bat that not very many players can do," said longtime Orioles catcher Rick Dempsey. "Not only was he a good power hitter, but he was a very good average hitter. He could spray the ball around, go the opposite way with power. He just had tremendous offensive ability."

Murray lost parts of three seasons to labor strikes in 1981, 1994 and 1995, which likely kept him from becoming only the fourth player in history to reach 2,000 career RBIs.

He didn't have to get there, however, for opposing pitchers to realize just how challenging a hitter he was.

"He had a presence about him when he came to the plate," said former White Sox pitcher Britt Burns. "He was strong and quick, one of those guys who's a great athlete. He was not just a one-dimensional guy who was strong or who could make contact. He could do both—often."

ABOVE: Eddie Murray drops his bat and charges to first after a game-winning hit. (Getty Images)

No. 11
Cap Anson

One of the most important factors in evaluating Cap Anson's career statistics is this: in his first seven years in the National League, he played a total of 586 games, an average of only 73 per season.

Given that information, the fact that Anson still ranks seventh on the all-time list for most hits in a career, third all-time in career RBIs and 14th all-time in doubles has a little extra meaning. Those career numbers earned him the 11th spot in the Rawlings rankings of the game's greatest hitters with a composite total of 54 points.

Anson is often overlooked on lists of the greatest all-time players because his career was spent entirely in the 1800s. He was the game's first legitimate star and is considered by most historians to be the most dominant baseball figure of the 19th century.

Anson signed a professional contract with Rockford of the National Association in 1872 at the age of 19, after spending one year at Notre Dame, where he helped bring the sport of baseball to that college campus.

When the National League was formed in 1876, Anson was one of the charter members of the Chicago White Stockings, who later changed their name to the Cubs. He starred with the team until 1898, also serving as the team's manager for most of that period.

Anson became the first player in major league history to reach 3,000 hits, hitting .300 or better 19 times and winning three batting titles. Under his lead-

ership Chicago won five pennants between 1880 and 1886.

Anson was the first player in history to record four doubles in a game and the first to hit five home runs in consecutive games. A right-handed hitter who stood six foot one and weighed 225 pounds, Anson led the NL in RBIs four times, on-base percentage four times and in doubles twice. Anson topped the 100-RBI mark five times and for his career averaged an RBI for every five at-bats.

When he retired as a player, Anson led all major league players in career games, hits, at-bats, doubles, RBIs and runs. His hits record was not broken for 20 years, until he was finally passed by Ty Cobb.

Anson actually is perhaps better known for the improvements and strategy he brought to the game of baseball more than for his own performance as a player. He is credited with inventing the hit-and-run play, was the first person to decide to use a pitching rotation, the first to use signals to get information to his fielders and batters and was the first manager to have his team travel south to practice and play exhibition games before the season began—the start of spring training.

He also was remembered for other reasons—he often said that when he died, he wanted his tombstone to read "Here lies a .300 hitter." Anson also was

OPPOSITE: Adrian "Cap" Anson, a legend of early baseball, finished his career with a .329 batting average. (AP/WWP)

ABOVE: Cap Anson—the first player in major league history to reach 3,000 hits. (Brace Photo)

the first baseball player in history to write his autobiography.

Another reason he is remembered today is that he was an admitted racist, who campaigned and did whatever he could to keep blacks from playing in the major leagues. In 1883, Anson refused to have the White Stockings play an exhibition game in Toledo because the Toledo club had a black catcher, Moses Fleetwood Walker. Anson finally backed down and played the game when he was told the White Stockings would not receive the gate receipts if the game was not played.

Four years later, in 1887, the New York Giants wanted to sign a black pitcher, George Stovey, but Anson led the campaign to prevent it and this time was successful. That led the major leagues to adopt a "gentleman's agreement" even though it was not in writing, that the major leagues would remain for whites only. That agreement prevailed until 1947 when Branch Rickey broke the color barrier by signing Jackie Robinson to play for the Brooklyn Dodgers.

OPPOSITE: Cap Anson was a charter member of the Chicago White Stockings. (Brace Photo)

No. 12 (Tie)

Barry Bonds

As one of only two active players to make the list of Rawlings' 25 greatest hitters of all time, there is no question Barry Bonds will be moving up in the rankings as he heads toward the end of a fabulous career.

The only question is how far he will climb.

Bonds enters the 2004 season tied with Frank Robinson as the 12th greatest hitter of all time on the Rawlings scale. He earned 49 points on the strength of ranking fourth all-time in career homers (658, two behind his godfather Willie Mays), 16th all-time in career RBIs (70 behind Robinson), 25th in career doubles (eight away from reaching the 18th place all-time, and 10th in career total bases.

The determining factors in how high Bonds will move up in all of the career statistical categories likely will be his age—he will celebrate his 40th birthday on July 24, 2004—and how much longer he wants to play. Already the single-season home run record holder with his 73-homer season in 2001, Bonds doesn't need to keep playing the game to earn his place in the record book or the Hall of Fame.

Still, he does have goals to shoot for, and it is not unrealistic to think he can surpass Hank Aaron's career mark of 755 homers. Bonds enters the 2004 season 98 homers away from breaking the record, and, having averaged 53 homers for his previous four years, could be only two years away from breaking Aaron's record.

There appears to be no sign of decline in Bonds's performance despite his age. He won his third consecutive MVP award in 2003, a season in which he also had to cope with the illness and death of his father, Bobby, which forced him to miss several games. Bonds's MVP was his sixth overall, the most in major league history.

Of the four major professional sports, only Kareem Abdul-Jabbar (NBA), Wayne Gretzky and Gordie Howe (NHL) have won as many or more MVP awards in their league. Abdul-Jabbar and Howe each also won six; Gretzky won nine.

"There has got to be a league somewhere on another planet where he could be an average guy," said Felipe Alou, Bonds's manager in 2003.

His longtime manager with the Giants, Dusty Baker, now the manager of the Cubs, once said of Bonds, "He comes from good stock. His dad was one hell of a player, you know. It's like child actors. You're around the set all your life. You're not nervous. You know what camera to look at, when to expand your lines. Barry has an overall intellect for the game."

As good a player as Bobby Bonds was, however, during his 14-year career in the majors, Barry definitely has passed him by. Combined, the Bondses hold

OPPOSITE: Barry Bonds hits the 500th home run of his career during the eighth inning against the Los Angeles Dodgers. (Jed Jacobsohn/ Getty Images)

"It's a different sound. He hits the ball harder than anybody I've ever seen."

—Atlanta manager Bobby Cox

the all-time father-son records for homers, RBIs and stolen bases.

Only four players in history have hit 300 or more homers and stolen 300 or more bases—Barry Bonds, Bobby Bonds, Willie Mays and Andre Dawson. Barry Bonds has done a little more—with his 500th career stolen base in 2003, he became the only member of the 500-homer, 500-stolen base club, just as he was the solo member of the 400-400 club.

The younger Bonds also is one of only three players, along with Jose Canseco and Alex Rodriguez, to hit 40 or more homers and steal 40 bases in a season. He has reached the 30-30 mark five times in his career. The only other person to make that same claim was his dad.

Barry Bonds's stolen bases have dropped off over the years, but his 45-homer season in 2003 was the seventh 40-plus season of his career and the fourth consecutive. He has topped the 30 mark in 13 of his 17 major league seasons, including the last 12 years in a row, which ties the major league record set by Jimmie Foxx. He has 64 career multi-homer games, third all-time behind Ruth and Mark McGwire.

The left-handed-hitting Bonds also has 11 career 100- or more RBI seasons, which ties the National League record set by Aaron. He hit .341 in 2003, fol-lowing his first batting championship season of .370 in 2002, and has now hit .300 or better for 10 seasons, including the last four in a row.

Along the way he also moved into second place all-time in walks, passing Ruth, and set the major league record for intentional walks, the ultimate sign of respect from opposing managers.

"It's a different sound," Atlanta manager Bobby Cox said in describing how Bonds hits the ball. "He hits the ball harder than anybody I've ever seen."

Bonds was not always a power hitter. Drafted by the Pirates out of Arizona State in the first round of the 1985 draft, Bonds played just 115 games in the minor leagues before making his major league debut in 1986. He was a leadoff hitter for his first seven years in the majors, hitting his first career homer on June 4, 1986 at Atlanta off the Braves' Craig McMurtry.

Bonds, a 12-time All-Star and 10-time starter, left the Pirates after the 1992 season and signed with the Giants as a free agent. He was part of a pennant-winning team for the first time in 2002, after losing three times in the NLCS with the Pirates, but saw his first World Series end in disappointment when the Giants lost to the Anaheim Angels, giving Bonds at least one other unfulfilled goal to try to reach before he walks away from the game.

OPPOSITE: Barry Bonds is honored at Pac Bell Park in San Francisco for breaking the single-season home run record on October 5, 2001. (Jed Jacobsohn/Getty Images)

No. 12 (Tie)

Frank Robinson

When the Cincinnati Reds traded Frank Robinson to the Baltimore Orioles at the end of the 1965 season, they said he was "an old 30." All he did the following year was win the Triple Crown, lead the Orioles to the world championship and become the first player in history to win the MVP award in both leagues.

Not bad for a player who supposedly was on the down side of his career.

Robinson continued to lead the Orioles for five more seasons, helping the team win three more pennants and another World Series, as he solidified his ranking among the game's greatest hitters of all time and enforced the position that the Reds had made one of the game's all-time worst trades.

In the Rawlings rankings, Robinson finished with 49 points, placing him in a tie for 12th place all-time with Barry Bonds, the highest ranked active player and one of just two active players to earn a spot in the top 25. Robinson ranks fifth all-time in career homers with 586, 15th all-time in career RBIs, and ninth all-time in career total bases.

Robinson starred for the Reds for 10 seasons, beginning with his NL Rookie of the Year campaign as a 20-year-old outfielder in 1956 when he tied the then rookie home run record with 38. Robinson had signed with the Reds' minor league system after a great high school career in Oakland, where he was a team-mate of Curt Flood and Vada Pinson in baseball and future Hall of Famer Bill Russell in basketball.

During his years in Cincinnati, Robinson averaged 33 homers and 100 RBIs a year, but that still didn't keep the Reds from deciding his best years were behind him. After the 1965 season, Robinson was traded by the Reds with Dick Simpson to Baltimore for Milt Pappas and Jack Baldschun.

He had won the MVP in the National League after leading the Reds to the 1961 pennant, and led the NL in slugging percentage for three consecutive years, but general manager Bill DeWitt still believed it was time to trade Robinson after he hit .296 with 33 homers and 113 RBIs in 1965.

The change of scenery did not affect Robinson's performance—in his first AL season he hit a career-high 49 homers, drove in a career-high 122 runs and won the batting championship with a .316 average. He then led the Orioles to a four-game sweep of the Dodgers in the World Series.

"He took terrific talent and made it even better with his intensity," said longtime Orioles second baseman Davey Johnson. "It has never been any secret that anyone who played against Frank hated him while the guys who played with him loved him."

OPPOSITE: Cincinnati Reds outfielder Frank Robinson shown here in this 1962 photo. (AP/WWP)

"Pitchers did me a favor when they knocked me down. It made me more determined. I wouldn't let that pitcher get me out. They say you can't hit if you're on your back, but I didn't hit on my back. I got up."

—Frank Robinson

Robinson topped the 30-homer mark 11 times in his career and drove in 100 or more runs six times while finishing the year hitting .300 or better nine times. An 11-time All-Star, Robinson was known for his intensity, his dislike of his opponents, his competitive desire to win and his tendency to challenge pitchers by crowding the plate. He was not afraid of getting hit by a pitch, or getting knocked down.

"Pitchers did me a favor when they knocked me down," Robinson said one time. "It made me more determined. I wouldn't let that pitcher get me out. They say you can't hit if you're on your back, but I didn't hit on my back. I got up."

Robinson would have won the 1962 NL batting title had the Giants and Dodgers not tied for the pennant. The teams played a three-game playoff, and the statistics counted as part of the regular season. Tommie Davis of the Dodgers used those games to raise his average to .346, four percentage points ahead of Robinson.

Robinson concluded his 21-year playing career as the player-manager of the Cleveland Indians in 1975. He hit the eighth and final opening day homer of his career that season, but had to answer more questions about being the first black man to serve as a manager in the major leagues.

A career .294 hitter, Robinson retired with 2,943 hits, 57 shy of the 3,000-hit club, and with 586 homers, just 14 away from being one of four players (at the time) to hit 600 homers. Some people urged him to continue his career to try to reach those milestones, but Robinson refused to do that.

"I played 21 years and if I didn't get those hits or home runs in 21 years, then I was not going to hang around two or three more years just to acquire numbers," he said.

Robinson believed he had already created enough numbers and celebrated enough special moments, such as the day in 1966 when he hit what might have been one of the longest homers in history.

Playing at Memorial Stadium in Baltimore, Robinson hit a pitch from Luis Tiant of the Indians out of the stadium, the first ball ever to leave that ballpark. The ball was later retrieved by a fan and the distance of the homer was estimated at 540 feet.

Robinson, who later went on to manage the Giants and Orioles, begins the 2004 season in his second year as manager of the Montreal Expos. He was elected to the Hall of Fame in 1982.

ABOVE: Fans look on as Frank Robinson gives them their money's worth. (AP/WWP)

No. 14
Cal Ripken Jr.

The first thing a baseball fan thinks of when he hears the name Cal Ripken Jr. is The Streak.

Ripken knows this his legacy will be playing more consecutive games than anyone in history, breaking Lou Gehrig's supposedly unbreakable record of 2,130 games in 1995—then playing 501 more games before his streak finally came to an end late in the 1998 season.

What people forget about the Baltimore legend, however, is that Ripken would not have played every game between May 30, 1982 and September 20, 1998—a span of 2,632 games—if he had not been a productive player on both offense and defense.

Because offense is what is being measured by these Rawlings rankings, Ripken earned the No. 14 spot on the all-time list solely through his offensive performance and not because of the streak—which puts him into a different place on another list of the game's all-time greats.

Ripken finished these rankings with 47 points on the strength of finishing 14th all-time in career hits, 19th all-time in career RBIs, 12th all-time in career doubles, and 12th all-time in career total bases.

All of those numbers, as well as his defensive performance, tend to be overlooked, however, because all anyone wants to talk about regarding Ripken is the streak, and that does him a great disservice.

"Whether your name is Gehrig, or Ripken, [Joe] DiMaggio or Jackie Robinson, or that of some young-ster who picks up his bat or puts on his glove, you are challenged by the game of baseball to do your very best day in and day out. That's all I've ever tried to do," Ripken once said.

Tutored by his father, Cal Ripken Sr., who for a while was his manager in Baltimore and also was a longtime Orioles coach, the younger Ripken was successful in his goal. He became one of only seven players in history to record 3,000 or more hits and 400 or more home runs before he retired in 2001. He became only the second player, following Carl Yazstremski, to do it while playing his entire career in the American League. The fact he did it playing shortstop for most of his career is even more impressive.

Ripken holds the all-time record for most home runs by a shortstop, 345 of his 431 career homers. His career total puts him fourth all-time among players who never won a home run title, trailing Rafael Palmeiro, Stan Musial and Dave Winfield.

During his distinguished career, Ripken produced five .300 seasons, topped the 100-RBI mark four times and hit 20 or more homers in a season 12 times, doing it for 10 consecutive years. He tops the Orioles' career charts for games, at-bats, runs, hits, doubles, home runs and RBI.

OPPOSITE: On the 3001st and final game of his career, Cal Ripken Jr. connects with a pitch at Camden Yards. (Doug Pensinger/Getty Images)

"It's extremely impressive that Cal was able to do something like this while playing shortstop. You have to have size and strength, which he obviously has. You have to have skill, and you have to have some luck. I have always thought that shortstops were the best athletes in the field, and this just reconfirms that."

—Shortstop Ozzie Smith

One of Ripken's contemporaries as a shortstop, but in the National League, was Ozzie Smith, who was impressed by The Streak—but more so by what Ripken was able to accomplish while playing every day.

"It's extremely impressive that Cal was able to do something like this while playing shortstop," Smith once said. "You have to have size and strength, which he obviously has. You have to have skill, and you have to have some luck. I have always thought that shortstops were the best athletes in the field, and this just reconfirms that."

Thought by some skeptics to be too tall at six foot, four inches to be a shortstop, Ripken proved his critics wrong right from the beginning of his career as he became the first player in history to win the Rookie of the Year award and the Most Valuable Player of the year award in consecutive seasons.

In 1982, he was honored as the top rookie after hitting .264 with 28 homers and 93 RBIs. The following year, he led the Orioles to the AL pennant and their only world championship during his career by hitting .318 with 27 homers and 102 RBIs.

From 1983 through 1986, Ripken led all major league shortstops in home runs, RBIs, runs and slugging percentage as he established himself as one of the game's greats.

Ripken played in 19 All-Star games during his career, making 17 consecutive starts, the last three at third base, and twice was named the game's MVP. He also was named to the All-Century team after the 1999 season.

Ripken won his second MVP award in 1991, but from that moment on began to be noticed almost exclusively because of the streak, creeping ever closer to Gehrig's record.

When major league players went on strike in 1994, and then were locked out at the start of the 1995 season, fans and many in baseball were worried Ripken's streak would fall short of Gehrig's, but he was back in the lineup when the games resumed and finally tied and passed Gehrig on September 5 and 6, 1995, at Camden Yards. Baseball executives were not shy in praising Ripken's role in helping bring disgruntled fans back to the ballpark after the strike, saying he had helped to "save" baseball.

Ripken continued to play, passing another consecutive games record set by a player from Japan, until September 20, 1982, when he walked into manager Ray Miller's office and told him to scratch his name from the lineup. Rookie Ryan Minor took Ripken's place at third that night, but no one will ever take Ripken's place in history.

ABOVE: Cal Ripken Jr. patiently awaits the pitch.
(Jed Jacobsohn/Getty Images)

No. 15
George Brett

If George Brett could pick any hitter to be at the plate with the game on the line, he would pick himself. A lot of other baseball people who coached Brett or coached against him during his 21-year career with the Kansas City Royals would give the same answer.

"If you want to say what was George's biggest asset, he was one of the best clutch hitters in the game," said his onetime manager and longtime friend, Whitey Herzog.

Sparky Anderson managed the Detroit Tigers and went up against Brett many times, which he never found to be an enjoyable experience.

"With Cincinnati [when he was managing the Reds] I used to walk the Giants' Willie McCovey all the time because he could just kill you," Anderson once said. "I thought I'd never treat another hitter that way, but I wound up doing it with George.

"It got to the point where, if the game was on the line, I told our pitchers not to throw a strike—never—roll the ball up there if you have to."

Brett earned that respect by his outstanding performance throughout his career, which included becoming the first hitter in history to win a batting title in three different decades, winning the AL championship in 1976, 1980 and 1990.

In the Rawlings rankings of the greatest hitters of all time, Brett finished at No. 15 with 43 points. He ranks 15th all-time in career hits, fifth all-time in career doubles and 15th all-time in career total bases.

Brett credited much of his success to his work with Royals hitting coach Charley Lau, who taught him the advantage of being able to hit to all fields, but also to his own self-confidence, believing in himself and his own ability. It wasn't through arrogance or cockiness, but just his knowledge of what needed to be done and of his own ability to do it.

"I trusted my work ethic and I trusted my swing," Brett once said. "It didn't always work, but I'll tell you what, if you go up there believing you're going to get a hit, at least you have a chance. If you go up there knowing you're not going to get a hit or not trying to convince yourself you're going to get a hit, you won't."

Never was Brett's confidence higher than in the 1980 season, when he mounted the most serious threat to hitting .400 since Ted Williams hit .406 39 years earlier. Brett enjoyed a 37-game hitting streak during the season and went into September hitting .403. He kept his average hovering around the magic number, despite the growing media attention and pressure, until September 20, when his average finally fell below .400. He finished the year at .390—a difference of only five hits, over the course of the season, away from joining that exclusive club.

Brett's performance nevertheless earned him the league MVP as he led the Royals to their first AL pen-

OPPOSITE: Kansas City Royal George Brett follows through beautifully. (Jonathan Daniel/Getty Images)

nant. Even though they lost the World Series to the Philadelphia Phillies, Brett was a standout performer, just as he was five years later when Kansas City finally won its first world championship by defeating the St. Louis Cardinals. In his combined World Series appearances, Brett posted a .373 average.

He also is remembered for his three-homer performance against Catfish Hunter in a playoff game and his clutch playoff homer off the Yankees' Goose Gossage.

Brett, a career .305 hitter during the regular season, became the only player in history to record 3,000 hits, 300 home runs, 600 doubles, 100 triples and steal 200 bases in his career. He was the only player other than Ty Cobb to lead his league in hits and triples in the same season. In 1979, he became only the sixth player in history to hit 20 or more doubles, triples and home runs in the same season.

The fact that the left-handed-hitting Brett made hitting look so easy was what impressed many of Brett's opponents, including fellow Hall of Famer Carl Yastrezmski.

"When I think of how hard I've worked at hitting and how many hours I've put into it, and then look at Brett making it look so easy, I'm amazed," Yastrezmski once said. "Yes, he makes hitting look easy."

Brett, who made his major league debut in 1973 and was one of the rare players who spent his entire career with one team, is the younger brother of Ken Brett, who pitched in the majors for 13 years. Two of their brothers also played in the minor leagues.

Brett led the Royals to six division championships in his career and was a 12-time All-Star. He topped the .300 mark 11 times and four years drove in 100 or more runs. He is the Royals' all-time leader in every career offensive category except stolen bases.

Brett was elected to the Hall of Fame in 1999, his first year of eligibility, receiving 98 percent of the vote.

OPPOSITE: George Brett—in typical fashion—connects yet again. (Rick Stewart/Getty Images)

No. 16
Paul Waner

Growing up on a farm in Oklahoma, Paul Waner and his younger brother Lloyd didn't have a regulation baseball or bat, so when they wanted to play, they had to make do with what they could find. More times than not, their "ball" was a broken corn cob, and the "bat" was a sawed-down broom handle.

The two brothers rose from that humble beginning to both become Hall of Famers, known by the nicknames of "Big Poison" and "Little Poison," a reference to their ages more than their size, since both were built of similar, small stature. Paul, three years older than Lloyd, stood about five feet, eight and a half inches tall and weighed less than 160 pounds.

Paul Waner was the more successful of the brothers, who spent 14 years together in the Pittsburgh outfield. He reached the majors in 1926 at the age of 23 to start a 20-year career and was a gifted hitter, primarily because of his great reflexes and his ability to often out-think a pitcher.

On the Rawlings scale of the game's all-time greatest hitters, Waner came in ranked 16th with a total score of 41.5 points. He ranks 16th on the all-time hits list, is tied for 10th in career doubles and is 10th all-time in triples. He never hit more than 15 homers in a season.

Born in 1903, Waner originally was a left-handed pitcher before he hurt his arm and switched to the outfield before beginning his minor league career with San Francisco in the Coast league.

Twice Waner led the National League in doubles and triples for a season, and he hit 50 or more doubles in three seasons. A left-handed batter, he used his great speed not only to beat out bunts and other infield hits, but to stretch line drives to the outfield gaps into doubles and triples.

Waner hit .336 as a rookie for the Pirates and improved his average to a league-leading .380 the next season, when he led Pittsburgh to the pennant and into the World Series, where the Pirates were swept by the Yankees in the only postseason appearance of Waner's career.

That batting title was the first of three for Waner, who also won the titles in 1934 with a .362 average and in 1936 with a .373 mark. Waner topped .300 for 12 consecutive seasons, six times surpassing .the 350 mark. He had 200 or more hits in a season eight times, a mark equaled by Ty Cobb and Pete Rose.

A lifetime .333 hitter who was second among National Leaguers in career hits behind Honus Wagner when he retired, Waner didn't look like much of a ballplayer on first impressions because of his size. Legendary Giants manager John McGraw was among those who were impressed.

A scout once told McGraw in describing Waner, "That little punk doesn't even know how to put on a

OPPOSITE: Paul Waner, with the Pirates for 14 seasons, is shown here wearing glasses in this April 13, 1940 photo. (AP/WWP)

"It isn't the bat. It's the man who's wielding it."

—Paul Waner

uniform." McGraw reportedly replied, "That little punk doesn't know how to put on a uniform, but he's removed three of my pitchers with line drives this week. I'm glad you didn't scout Christy Mathewson."

Part of Waner's ability could no doubt be traced to his terrific eyesight, which might have been improved by hitting those broken corn cobs on the Oklahoma farm. He even wrote a book about hitting, stressing his theory that hitters would be more successful if they faced a pitcher with both eyes instead of standing parallel to the plate, having one eye hidden behind his shoulder, which is a more conventional stance.

Waner struck out only 376 times in his career, out of more than 9,400 at-bats. He never struck out more than 34 times in a season.

"Why shouldn't he be a great hitter?" said Brooklyn manager Wilbert Robinson. "He's got eyes like a cat."

In order to prove to some of his doubting teammates that it was not important what bat you used, Waner one time intentionally told the Pittsburgh bat boy to give him a different bat every time he came up during a game. He went four for five.

"It isn't the bat," Waner said. "It's the man who's wielding it."

Elected to the Hall of Fame in 1952, 15 years before his brother joined him in Cooperstown, Waner also was not above playing games with opposing catchers and pitchers. Legend has it that during one game at Wrigley Field in Chicago in 1932, he told Cubs catcher Gabby Hartnett that he had not been able to get much sleep the night before, so he would appreciate it if the Cubs' pitchers would not throw the ball close to his head, because he might not be able to get out of the way.

Hartnett said the Cubs would honor that request, and then watched Waner pound out four doubles in the game.

In his final professional season, as a minor-leaguer playing at the age of 43 in 1946, Waner still hit .325.

When he began having trouble with his eyesight late in his career, then-Boston manager Casey Stengel quipped, "Paul has probably been hitting from memory for the last couple of years."

ABOVE: Paul Waner, left, with brother Lloyd, made up two-thirds of the Pittsburgh Pirates' outfield for two decades and were both elected to the Hall of Fame. (AP/WWP)

No. 17
Jimmie Foxx

Ever since Babe Ruth slugged his record-breaking 60th home run in 1927, the world acknowledged his greatness and his accomplishment for setting one of baseball's most storied records and holding it until 1961, when Roger Maris hit 61 homers.

If not for construction changes at two major league stadiums and Mother Nature, however, Ruth's mark might have stood for only five years instead of 34—and when Maris hit his 61st homer, he still would have been seven homers behind the total hit by Jimmie Foxx.

Foxx, the power-hitting first baseman of the Philadelphia Athletics, hit 58 homers in 1932, but experts and historians agree that the slugger with huge biceps and forearms lost eight potential homers that season because of the addition of screens to Sportsman's Park in St. Louis and Municipal Stadium in Cleveland, neither of which was in place when Ruth set the homer mark five years earlier.

Studies found that Foxx hit five balls into the screen in front of the right field pavilion at Sportsman's Park, which would have been homers in any season prior to 1932. A screen was also erected that year in front of the left field stands in Cleveland, and Foxx hit three balls into that screen, which would have been homers in any previous year. Losing those homers, plus playing several weeks with a sprained wrist in the second half of the season, cost Foxx his chance at Ruth's record.

Foxx also lost two would-be homers that year when games were rained out before they could become official.

Foxx was used to following in Ruth's shadow, however. Still, his accomplishments, not just in 1932 but for his entire 20-year career, earned him the 17th spot on the Rawlings rankings of the game's all-time greatest hitters. Foxx collected 41 points, ranking 12th all time in home runs with 534, seventh all-time in RBIs; and 18th all-time in total bases. It also earned him a spot in the Hall of Fame. He was elected in 1951.

For a 12-year period, between 1929 and 1940, Foxx was the dominant slugger in the game, hitting at least 30 homers and driving in 100 or more runs every season. His streak of driving in 100 or more runs for 13 consecutive years is a record also achieved by Lou Gehrig.

Foxx was more than just a slugger, however, as he also won two American League batting titles and should have won a third, also in 1932.

Foxx hit .364 that season, but finished second in the batting race when the title was given to a player who finished three percentage points higher but only had 400 at-bats. Foxx would have won the Triple

OPPOSITE: The legendary Jimmie Foxx is shown here gripping his bat in his Philadelphia Athletics uniform. (Hulton Archive/Getty Images)

"I never saw **anyone** hit a baseball harder than Foxx."

—Ted Williams

Crown if he had claimed the batting title, also leading the league in RBIs (with 169) and homers (58).

Foxx did win the Triple Crown the following year, hitting .356 with 48 homers and 163 RBIs.

One of the pitchers who was scared to face Foxx, and admitted it, was Hall of Famer Lefty Gomez.

"He was the only hitter I ever saw who could hit balls off his fist and still get them out of the park," Gomez said. "He had muscles on his muscles."

One of Foxx's longest homers came in 1937 off Gomez, which reached the third deck at Yankee Stadium and still had enough velocity to break a chair. The blast was later estimated at 550 feet.

"I don't know how far it went," Gomez said that day, "but I do know it takes 45 minutes to walk up there."

Foxx also hit a homer at the old Comiskey Park in Chicago that cleared the double-decked stadium, a record-setting blast.

Like Gomez, there are many Hall of Famers who consider Foxx the right-handed equivalent of Ruth. One who was solidly in Foxx's corner was Ted Williams, Foxx's teammate with the Red Sox from 1939 to 1942.

"I never saw anyone hit a baseball harder than Foxx," Williams said.

Foxx developed his strength as a young boy working on a Maryland farm and actually made his major league debut with Philadelphia in 1925 at the age of 17 after he was recommended to Connie Mack by Home Run Baker. It took Foxx a couple of years to settle into a regular position, at first base, but there was no doubt about his ability to hit.

In addition to his two batting titles, he won four home run crowns—competing against Ruth, Hank Greenberg and other sluggers—and was named the AL Most Valuable Player three times. Twice he topped 50 homers, and his career total of 534 ranked second all-time to Ruth for many years. He became the youngest player to reach the 500-homer plateau when he clubbed that homer at the age of 33 in 1940.

Foxx led the Athletics to three pennants and two world championships, also competing against the powerful Yankees before the financially strapped Athletics traded him to Boston in 1936.

OPPOSITE: Jimmie Foxx is shown here hitting his 495th major-league homer. (AP/WWP)

No. 18
Lou Gehrig

As great a player as he was during his career, Lou Gehrig never received as much attention and praise as he should have received. He seemed to always be in the shadow of Babe Ruth, literally and figuratively, or had other obstacles blocking his road to fame.

On one of the greatest days of his or anyone's career—when Gehrig hit four consecutive home runs on June 3, 1932 at Shibe Park in Philadelphia against the Athletics, and narrowly missed a fifth homer—the headlines in the New York newspapers the following day were about the sudden resignation of John McGraw as manager of the Giants.

"I'm not a headline guy," Gehrig admitted one time. "I'm just the guy who's in there every day, the fellow who follows Babe in the batting order."

There is no way to measure, of course, what impact Gehrig had on the career of Babe Ruth, who batted in front of Gehrig during most of his glory days with the Yankees. There is no doubt, however, that Ruth's performance had an impact on Gehrig.

Just one example of Ruth's impact on Gehrig came in 1931, when Gehrig set the American League record of 184 RBIs. Forty-seven times that year Gehrig came to bat with no RBI possibilities other than hitting a home run himself because Ruth had just cleared the bases with a home run.

On the Rawlings scale of the game's greatest all-time hitters, Gehrig comes in at number 18 with a total of 40 points. He ranks 20th all-time in career homers with 493, is fourth all-time in career RBIs with 1,995 and is 14th all-time in total bases with 5,060.

"No man could ever hit a ball off the right field or left field wall harder than he did," said longtime Yankees catcher Bill Dickey. "He was a left-handed hitter, but he hit line drives off the left center field wall that no right-handed hitter could accomplish."

Added another teammate, Joe DiMaggio, "He was the most powerful hitter I ever saw."

The son of German immigrants who worked at Columbia University in New York, Gehrig got his baseball start in high school in New York and was part of the city championship team that traveled to Chicago to play a game against the city champions of Chicago at Wrigley Field. Gehrig won the game for the New York squad with a home run in the ninth inning that cleared the stadium.

He went on to star at Columbia and was discovered by a Yankees scout who signed him after watching him play only two games. Gehrig received a $1,500 bonus and a $3,000 contract for the remainder of the 1923 season.

Gehrig played sparingly his first two years with the Yankees, but moved into the starting lineup on June 1, 1925 when regular first baseman Wally Pipp

OPPOSITE: Baseball great Lou Gehrig in action at Yankee Stadium. (AP/WWP)

"No man could ever hit a ball off the right field or left field wall harder than he did. He was a left-handed hitter, but he hit line drives off the left center field wall that no right-handed hitter could accomplish."

—Yankees catcher Bill Dickey

was suffering from a headache. Gehrig did not come out of the lineup for almost 14 years, setting a then-record of playing in 2,130 consecutive games.

Gehrig's presence in the lineup was so taken for granted that he was within about 60 games of breaking the then-consecutive game streak of 1,307 games set by Everett Scott before it was discovered by a New York sportswriter that Gehrig had played in every game for eight years.

The streak became Gehrig's legacy, as did the illness that ultimately ended the streak and claimed his life. Gehrig was ill at the beginning of the 1939 season but kept playing until May 2, when he asked manager Joe McCarthy to keep him out of the lineup for a game at Detroit. Babe Dahlgreen replaced him.

Gehrig had kept the streak alive for 14 seasons by playing through a broken thumb, a broken rib, a broken toe, a twisted back, colds, lumbago and headaches. He could not play through a disease, however.

Six weeks after the streak ended, after an examination at the Mayo Clinic, it was determined that Gehrig was suffering from amyotrophic lateral sclerosis, ALS, which now has come to be known more commonly as "Lou Gehrig's disease."

Gehrig's career was over at the age of 35, and just over two years later, 17 days before his 38th birthday, Gehrig was dead.

Ironically, the streak and his death from ALS became the two most widely known facts about Gehrig, which once again denied him the headlines he should have received for his performance on the field.

A career .340 hitter who won the Triple Crown in 1934, Gehrig tied a record by driving in 100 or more runs for 13 consecutive years. Seven times he drove in 150 or more runs, and he averaged .92 RBIs a game for his 16-year career. During his 13-year 100-plus RBI streak, Gehrig averaged 147 RBIs a year.

Gehrig's 493 career homers included a record 23 grand slams but did not include his 10 World Series homers. He topped 40 homers in five seasons and also hit 40 or more doubles seven times and 10 or more triples eight times. He played in seven World Series, helping the Yankees win six world championships. His composite World Series numbers included a .361 average and 34 RBIs to go with the 10 homers.

He led the AL in RBIs four times, led in home runs twice and topped 400 total bases five times. A typical season for Gehrig was 1927, when he hit .373 with 47 homers and 175 RBIs, but saw Ruth get all of the headlines because of his record-setting 60 home runs.

The customary five-year wait for election to the Hall of Fame was waived when Gehrig died, and he was elected in 1939.

OPPOSITE: A smiling Lou Gehrig poses for the camera. (Hulton Archive/Getty Images)

No. 19
Dave Winfield

Not many athletes have the career options Dave Winfield had available to him when he was coming out of the University of Minnesota.

A baseball and basketball star for the Golden Gophers, Winfield was drafted by the San Diego Padres in baseball and by the Atlanta Hawks of the NBA and the Utah Stars of the old American Basketball Association. In addition, even though he did not play one down of college football, he was selected by his hometown team, the Minnesota Vikings of the NFL. He is the only athlete to be drafted by teams in those three professional sports.

A six foot, six inch gifted athlete, Winfield likely would have succeeded in any of the three sports, but believing his best opportunity was in baseball, that was the sport he chose—and it was obvious early that he made the right decision.

Winfield is one of a handful of players who never spent a day in the minor leagues, joining the Padres directly from the college campus. In 56 games as a rookie in 1973, Winfield hit .277 with three homers and 12 RBIs. In his first full year in 1974, Winfield hit .265 with 20 homers and 75 RBIs—displaying the talent that was to make him a Hall of Famer, a member of the class of 2001.

On the Rawlings rankings of the game's greatest hitters, Winfield finished at No. 19 with 39.5 points. He ranks 25th all-time in career homers, 19th in career hits, 13th in career RBIs, tied with Joe Medwick for 22nd all-time in career doubles, and 11th all-time in career total bases.

Winfield is one of just four players—along with Hank Aaron, Eddie Murray and Ty Cobb—to rank in the top 25 in five of the six categories used to compile the Rawlings rankings. The only player to rank in the top 25 in all six categories was Stan Musial.

Winfield might have been born to be a star, coming into the world on October 3, 1951, the same day Bobby Thomson hit his pennant-winning homer for the New York Giants against the Dodgers. He became one of the most talented prep athletes in the history of St. Paul, Minnesota, and turned down an offer from the Baltimore Orioles when he was drafted out of high school in 1969 to accept a baseball scholarship to Minnesota.

Winfield was primarily a pitcher in college, until he hurt his shoulder and had to begin logging more time in the outfield. As a senior he led Minnesota to the College World Series, and even though the Gophers lost in the semifinals, he was named the Series MVP.

Despite playing for the lowly Padres, Winfield was able to establish himself as a gifted player. He hit 20 or more homers in five of his seven years in San Diego and enjoyed his best season in 1979, when he

OPPOSITE: California outfielder Dave Winfield watches his shot sail across the field. (Lonnie Major/Getty Images)

"Good hitters don't just go up and swing. They always have a plan. Call it an educated deduction. **You visualize.** You're like a good negotiator. You know what you have, you know what he has. Then you try to work it out."

—Dave Winfield

hit .308 with 34 homers and led the National League with 118 RBIs. It was the only time he led his league in a Triple Crown category during his 22-year career. It also was the first of three 30-homer seasons for Winfield, a career .283 hitter who topped the .300 mark four times.

Winfield ranks third among hitters with the most career homers who never led his league in homers in a single season, hitting 465, 10 fewer than Musial, and trailing Rafael Palmeiro. The closest he came to a batting title was after he signed as a free agent with the Yankees, when he hit .340 in 1984 but lost the title by three points to his Yankees teammate, Don Mattingly.

For a 15-year period between 1977 and 1992, Winfield averaged 99 RBIs a season.

Winfield credited much of his success to preparation, knowing what he was trying to do in every at-bat.

"Good hitters don't just go up and swing," he said once. "They always have a plan. Call it an educated deduction. You visualize. You're like a good negotiator. You know what you have, you know what he has. Then you try to work it out."

With the Yankees, Winfield found himself in constant feuds with owner George Steinbrenner. De-

spite success in the regular season—becoming the first Yankee to drive in 100 or more runs in five consecutive seasons since Joe DiMaggio—the Yankees reached the World Series only once during Winfield's 10 seasons with the team. In that 1981 Series against the Dodgers, Winfield hit just .045.

His chance for World Series redemption came 11 years later, playing with Toronto in 1992, when his double in Game 6 drove in the winning run and gave the Blue Jays their first championship.

Winfield completed his career in 1995 as one of only three players to record 3,000 hits, hit 450 homers and steal 200 bases. The other members of that club are Aaron and Willie Mays. The only players with more hits and home runs than Winfield are Aaron, Mays, Murray and Musial.

Winfield also is one of only three players to appear in more than 1,000 games in each league, along with Bob Boone and Frank Robinson.

A 12-time All-Star, the right-handed-hitting Winfield showed his desire to succeed when he missed the 1989 season after back surgery but came back the following year at the age of 38, allowing him to reach the 3,000-hit and 400-homer career marks. He hit for the cycle on June 24, 1991, becoming at 39 years old the oldest player to ever complete that feat.

OPPOSITE: Fierce Yankee Dave Winfield is prepared to unload everything he's got. (Rick Stewart/Getty Images)

No. 20
Paul Molitor

For much of the first half of his career, Paul Molitor was not as worried about the opposing pitcher as he was about staying healthy enough to remain in the Milwaukee Brewers' lineup.

Molitor was on the disabled list 10 times in the first 10 years he played in the major leagues, missing nearly the equivalent of three complete seasons because of a variety of injuries.

Molitor topped the .300 mark only three times before his 30th birthday, and only twice in his first 10 years in the majors was he able to play more than 140 games in a season.

It was in his 10th year, however, 1987, that Molitor finally began to display the form that was to lead him into the Hall of Fame and onto the Rawlings rankings of the greatest hitters of all time. Molitor ranks as the 20th best hitter of all time on the Rawlings scale, finishing with 37.5 points.

Molitor ranks ninth all-time in career hits, 10th all-time in career doubles and 21st all-time in career total bases.

Despite playing just 118 games in 1987, Molitor led the AL with 114 runs scored and 41 doubles while hitting .353. That was good enough for a second place finish in the batting race, 10 percentage points behind the Red Sox' Wade Boggs. During that summer Molitor put together a 39-game hitting streak, the longest streak in the American League since Joe DiMaggio set the record by hitting in 56 consecutive games in 1941.

Molitor was finally repaying the faith the Brewers had in making him their first-round pick in the 1977 draft, after his junior year at the University of Minnesota, the third overall choice in the draft. Molitor had been selected in the 28th round by the St. Louis Cardinals after high school, but he elected to accept a college scholarship instead of signing a pro contract.

That came three years later, and after just 64 games in the minor leagues, Molitor found himself as the opening day shortstop for the Brewers in 1978 because of an injury to Robin Yount. When Yount returned, Molitor moved to second base, and he also played third base and the outfield before settling in as a designated hitter for much of the second half of his career.

One of the few early highlights of Molitor's career with the Brewers came when the team won the AL pennant in 1982 and Molitor, playing his first World Series game, went five for five against the Cardinals to tie a record for most hits in a game.

His real chance at World Series history came 11 years later, when playing with Toronto. He was named the Series MVP for hitting .418 with six extra-base hits, including two homers, driving in eight runs, and scoring 10 runs to lead the Blue Jays to their second consecutive world championship.

OPPOSITE: Minnesota Twin Paul Molitor in action during spring training. (David Seelig/Getty Images)

"You have a feeling that **anything might happen** when he's at bat, and it usually does. When he hits the ball, it has a good chance of being in the hole somewhere."

—Former manager Cito Gaston

Molitor signed with the Blue Jays after a 15-year run in Milwaukee, and he enjoyed some special moments in Toronto. During the 1993 regular season, Molitor drove in 111 runs, topping the 100 mark for the first time in his career. At 37, he became the oldest player in history to drive in 100 runs for the first time. He also hit a career-best 22 homers and batted .332, finishing second in the batting race for the second time in his career. He also finished second in the league's MVP voting.

Molitor's manager that year, Cito Gaston, was among his leading believers.

"You have a feeling that anything might happen when he's at bat," Gaston said, "and it usually does. When he hits the ball, it has a good chance of being in the hole somewhere."

After finally finding a way to stay healthy and in the lineup, Molitor's success rate definitely increased.

From 1988 through 1997, Molitor led all major-leaguers with 1,811 hits, an average of 181 a season. After celebrating his 35th birthday in 1991, Molitor had three of his four 200-hit seasons, twice scored 100 runs and drove in 100 runs for the only two times in his career—despite having two of those seasons shortened because of players' strikes.

A right-handed hitter who was able to hit the ball to all fields, Molitor was a seven-time All-Star. He finished his 21-year career with a .306 average, topping the .300 mark 12 times. He led the AL in hits three times.

In 1996, when he celebrated his 40th birthday, Molitor became the first player since Sam Rice in 1930 to have 200 hits when he was 40, leading the league for the final time with 225 hits. He hit .341 that season and followed that by hitting .305 in 1997 when he was 41 years old.

Molitor finished his career as only the fifth player in history to record 3,000 hits and steal 500 bases, joining Ty Cobb, Honus Wagner, Eddie Collins and Lou Brock.

Longtime opponent Mark Langston was once asked what pitch Molitor couldn't hit, and he replied, "Ball four, and you'd better roll it."

Molitor was hired by the Seattle Mariners to serve as their hitting coach in 2004, the same year he will be inducted into baseball's Hall of Fame.

**ABOVE: Paul Molitor adds a hit to his impressive career.
(Al Bello/Getty Images)**

No. 21
Rafael Palmeiro

Rafael Palmeiro has very quietly earned his place on the list of the greatest hitters in baseball. So quietly, in fact, that he doesn't want to include himself in the company of the game's greats.

Palmeiro is one of just eight players in history with 500 or more homers, 2,500 or more hits and 500 or more doubles. Six of the players who belong to that club are in the Hall of Fame—Hank Aaron, Willie Mays, Eddie Murray, Frank Robinson, Babe Ruth and Ted Williams. The other player will be there five years after he retires—Barry Bonds.

"When you talk about guys like Ruth and Williams and [Mickey] Mantle, I'm not as good as they were," Palmeiro said the night he hit his 500th career homer. "Those guys were the greatest of all time. I've just been able to scrape together some good years and stayed healthy and gotten there. I don't put myself in some of those guys' group. They're the best of all time."

Despite Palmeiro's reluctance, he does belong in that category, finishing as the 21st best hitter of all time in the Rawlings rankings with 35.5 points. He ranks 13th all-time in career homers, 20th all-time in career RBIs, tied for 18th all-time in career doubles and 17th all-time in career total bases.

As one of only two active players to make the top 25 rankings, Palmeiro has a good chance of moving even higher in those categories in 2004. He rejoins the Baltimore Orioles, where he played from 1994 through 1998, for his 16th season in the major leagues.

Palmeiro enters this season in select company in other career categories as well. He has hit 35 or more homers and driven in 100 or more runs for the last nine seasons, tying Jimmie Foxx for the major league record for the most consecutive years of reaching those plateaus. The only players with longer streaks of hitting 30 or more homers in consecutive seasons are Foxx and Bonds, who both did it 12 years in a row. The other three hitters who did it for nine consecutive years were Lou Gehrig, Eddie Mathews and Mike Schmidt.

In 2003, Palmeiro hit 38 homers and drove in 112 runs for Texas, the 10th 100-RBI season of his career. He has hit 37 or more homers in 10 of the past 11 years, and for the 10 years between 1993 and 2002, Palmeiro hit 395 homers, drove in 1,154 runs and had 1,666 hits. That computes to an average of 39 homers, 115 RBIs and 166 hits a season.

Among active players, the 39-year-old Palmeiro ranks third in career homers, behind Bonds and Sammy Sosa; ranks second in career RBIs behind Bonds; ranks second in career hits behind Rickey Henderson; leads active players in career doubles, and ranks second to Bonds in career total bases.

Palmeiro enters the 2004 season 220 hits shy of joining Aaron, Mays and Murray as the only hitters in

OPPOSITE: Rafael Palmeiro is shown here hitting his 500th career home run during a game against the Cleveland Indians. (Ronald Martinez/Getty Images)

"He's the most underrated hitter ever, in my opinion."

—Former Yankees pitcher David Wells

history with both 3,000 career hits and 500 career homers.

Palmeiro also holds the career record for most homers by a hitter whose last name starts with P and has hit the most homers in history without ever leading his league in homers for one season.

The Chicago Cubs expected Palmeiro to be a great hitter when they drafted him in the first round in 1985 out of Mississippi State, where he had earned All-America honors three times and was a teammate of future major-leaguers Will Clark and Bobby Thigpen. Deciding that his future was at first base and already having Mark Grace to play that position, the Cubs traded Palmeiro to Texas after the 1988 season.

By the following year, 1990, Palmeiro was on his way to becoming a star, posting the first of five .300 seasons he would put together in a 10-year span. It didn't take his fellow American Leaguers long to begin noticing him.

"He's the most underrated hitter ever, in my opinion," said former Yankees pitcher David Wells.

Added New York catcher Jorge Posada, "He's always had that left-handed swing you want to copy. He's got a real smooth swing and he's never off-bal-ance. He's always on top of the ball. I just like watching him hit."

One of the few unfulfilled goals in Palmeiro's baseball life is to play for a world championship club. He has never played in the World Series, twice losing in the League Championship Series in his first stint with the Orioles.

Palmeiro credits much of his success in the game to the work he put in with his father when he was a young boy. Palmeiro, his parents and two of his brothers fled his native Cuba in 1971, when he was six years old, and settled in Miami.

"My dad was the force behind me early on," Palmeiro once said. "He was just infatuated with baseball. He was the one that basically taught me how to play the game. He gave a lot of his time working out with me, practicing and taking me to a lot of different games. It was hard work between both of us.

"By watching him, I learned to work for the things that I wanted to achieve. He made time every day after work. He worked in construction most of his life, and he'd come home about 4:00, 4:30 and eat something, change his clothes, then we'd go to the ballpark. Every day. He pushed me as hard as he could and kept me focused."

ABOVE: A humble Rafael Palmeiro hits his way onto the stage of other baseball greats such as Babe Ruth, Hank Aaron, and few others. (Ronald Martinez/Getty Images)

No. 22 (Tie)
Nap Lajoie

Nap Lajoie was involved in one of the biggest disputes in major league history, a battle that still was raging more than 70 years after it happened.

The dispute in question concerned the champion of the 1910 American League batting race between Lajoie and Ty Cobb. Almost everyone in the league, including Cobb's own teammates on the Tigers, were rooting for Lajoie, the star second baseman of the Cleveland Indians.

The race went down to the final day of the season. The Indians were playing a doubleheader against the Browns in St. Louis. Browns manager Jack O'Connor was one of the people in the league who disliked Cobb, and he was determined to do whatever he could to help Lajoie win the batting title. What he did was order his third baseman to play back, allowing Lajoie the opportunity to bunt the ball down the line and beat it out for a hit.

When Lajoie did just that, beating out seven bunts for hits that day, he and everybody else around the league thought he had won the batting title and the new Chalmers automobile that went with the title. When O'Connor's role in trying to decide the race was discovered, he was fired.

The dispute was far from over, however. A sportswriter came to Cobb's aid and changed a call on a play from earlier in the season, taking an error away and awarding Cobb another hit, which put him ahead of Lajoie one more time.

The race might have ended there, but more than 70 years later, research by *The Sporting News* revealed that Cobb had actually been credited for two extra hits when one game from that season had mistakenly been entered in the record book twice. The debate reached the commissioner's office, but he refused to change the original results.

Lajoie, of course, would not have been in that battle with Cobb had he not been a gifted hitter, good enough to earn 34 points on the Rawlings scale of the game's greatest hitters, finishing in a tie for 22nd on the all-time list with Mel Ott.

Seventy-seven years after he retired, Lajoie still ranks 13th on the all-time hits list with 3,242, sixth all-time in doubles with 657 and 25th all-time in RBIs.

"Lajoie was one of the most rugged hitters I ever faced," said the legendary Cy Young. "He'd take your leg off with a line drive, turn the third baseman around like a swinging door and powder the hand of the left fielder."

The Philadelphia Phillies did not know how good a player they were getting when they signed Lajoie off a semipro Falls River, Massachusetts, team in 1896.

OPPOSITE: Baseball great Nap Lajoie spent 21 years as a major-leaguer and ended his career in 1916 with a lifetime batting average of .339. (AP/WWP)

> # "Lajoie was one of the most rugged hitters I ever faced. He'd take your leg off with a line drive, turn the third baseman around like a swinging door and powder the hand of the left fielder."
>
> —Cy Young

Their scout had actually gone to watch and hopefully sign one of Lajoie's teammates, but came back with Lajoie as well.

The son of Canadian immigrants who had moved to Rhode Island when Lajoie was a boy, his first job was working in a textile mill. At the time he signed with the Phillies, he was working as a taxi driver with a horse and buggy while playing baseball on the weekends.

Lajoie became a star with the Phillies and by 1900 was making the National League's maximum salary of $2,400 a year. When the rival American League was formed in 1901 and included a team in Philadelphia, the A's raided the Phillies and signed several players, including Lajoie, who received $4,000 a year.

All Lajoie did that year was set the AL record for the highest batting average in a season, .426, which still stands today. He also won the Triple Crown by leading the new league in homers and RBIs.

The Phillies were so upset they went to court and received an injunction prohibiting Lajoie from playing for "another Philadelphia team." Instead of losing him back to the NL, American League presi-

dent Ban Johnson assigned Lajoie's contract to the Cleveland Indians, and he stayed there for all but the final two years of his career, when he returned to the A's.

Lajoie did have to sit out all of the Indians' games in Philadelphia because sheriff's deputies routinely met the train when it arrived in town, trying to serve a warrant against him.

Lajoie enjoyed a great career with the Indians, posting a .338 career average. He drove in 100 or more runs four times and led the AL in hits four times. His average topped the .300 mark in 16 of his 21 seasons and reached .350 twice.

The respect he received from opposing managers and players was almost universal. He holds one particular spot in baseball history—on May 23, 1901, Lajoie became the first major league hitter in history to be intentionally walked with the bases loaded.

Lajoie also served as the player-manager of the Indians from 1904-1909, a period in which the team was referred to as the "Naps" almost as often as they were called the Indians.

Lajoie was elected to the Hall of Fame in 1937.

OPPOSITE: Nap Lajoie is shown here in this 1912 photo. Lajoie was elected into the Baseball Hall of Fame in 1937. (AP/WWP)

No. 22 (Tie)
Mel Ott

When John McGraw took his first look at a 16-year-old ballplayer named Mel Ott, he immediately decided to keep the five-foot-nine 170-pounder with his New York Giants rather than send him to a minor league team.

It wasn't that Ott was so far advanced at that tender age that McGraw knew he belonged in the majors; it was that Ott had such an unorthodox batting style that McGraw knew if he sent Ott back to the minors, somebody would try to change it. He did not want that to happen.

So McGraw kept Ott sitting next to him on the Giants' bench for much of the next two years, although Ott did make his major league debut at the age of 17. By the time Ott was 19, he had hit 18 homers in the majors. The next season, at the age of 20, Ott hit 42 homers and drove in 151 runs.

The unique batting style saw the left-handed-hitting Ott raise his right, or front, leg into the air as the pitcher was winding up. He raised his leg about knee high, then brought it down as his bat was going back and his swing and planting the leg all seemed to come in one motion.

The kick was a timing device, helping Ott know when to begin his swing in order to generate the greatest possible power. The style of hitting worked well enough for him to hit 511 career homers and tie for the number 22 spot on the Rawlings rankings of the greatest hitters of all time.

Ott collected 40 points, the same as Nap Lajoie, on the strength of ranking 18th in career home runs in the majors, 10th in career RBIs and 16th in total bases.

Ott once said he didn't know any other way to hit, and he knew if somebody had tried to alter his approach he would not have been nearly as successful.

"I got my main power from my back foot," he once said. "With my right foot off the ground, I wouldn't be caught flat-footed. I had a better chance to wait on the pitch."

The ability to wait on the pitch made him a terrific dead-pull hitter, which worked to his great advantage in the Polo Grounds, where the Giants played their home games. The right field fence was only 257 feet away from home plate, and Ott hit 325 of his 511 career homers at home. He led the Giants in home runs for 18 consecutive seasons between 1928 and 1945.

The journey which led Ott to the Giants, especially at such an early age, was unusual. Ott was born and raised in Louisiana, and by the time he was a teenager, he was a very gifted ballplayer. He ended up playing on a semipro team in New Orleans owned by a wealthy businessman, Harry Williams, who happened to be friends with both McGraw, the manager of the Giants, and Connie Mack, the manager of the Philadelphia Athletics.

OPPOSITE: Mel Ott shows off his batting stance in this March 8, 1933 photo. (AP/WWP)

"I can't name a player who has exerted as strong an influence upon so many games as Mel."

—Pittsburgh third baseman Pie Traynor

It was Williams who contacted McGraw and arranged for Ott to join the Giants. Why he picked McGraw and not Mack was never revealed. Williams was on his way to Europe and mailed Ott a penny postcard telling him to report to McGraw and the Giants at the Polo Grounds. Ott thought the postcard was a joke and ignored it.

Several weeks later, when Williams returned from Europe, he found out Ott was still in New Orleans and repeated his instructions for him to join the Giants. This time Ott believed him.

It was a lucky break for the Giants, who saw Ott win five NL home run titles in a seven-year period between 1932 and 1938. He hit 30 or more homers eight times in his career and drove in 100 or more runs nine times. He was the first NL hitter to surpass 500 home runs for his career, and for many years he ranked third on the all-time list behind Babe Ruth and Jimmie Foxx.

Ott also posted a .300 or better average 10 times and also walked 100 or more times in 10 different seasons. He was often walked with runners already on first and second because the opposing manager did not want to give up a two- or three-run homer.

The worst example of opposing managers walking Ott came on the final day of the 1929 season, when the Philadelphia Phillies did not want him catching their own Chuck Klein for the home run title. The Phillies walked Ott intentionally five times in the game, including once with the bases loaded. Klein finished with 43 homers, Ott with 42.

Ott also spent six years as the player-manager of the Giants, and during his time with the club he helped the Giants win three pennants and one World Series. His 10th-inning home run in the final game won the 1933 Series for New York.

"I can't name a player who has exerted as strong an influence upon so many games as Mel," said longtime Pittsburgh third baseman Pie Traynor.

When he retired, Ott held the National League career records for home runs, RBIs, runs and walks. He also had a record 49 multihomer games in his career.

Ott was elected to the Hall of Fame in 1951. He was only 49 when he was killed in a car accident in Mississippi in 1958.

ABOVE: Mel Ott, in typical fashion, is shown here
raising his right foot before he hammers the ball.
(AP/WWP)

No. 24
Ted Williams

Most books that have been written about the history of baseball rank Ted Williams as one of the, if not *the* greatest hitter of all time. On the Rawlings scale, however, Williams comes in only as number 24.

The numbers are correct. Williams totaled 32.5 points based on his 14th spot all-time in career home runs (tied with Willie McCovey), his 12th place all-time in career RBIs, and his 19th spot all-time for career total bases. There is a reason, however, to look beyond those numbers.

No hitter in the history of baseball lost more than Williams because of his military service during World War II and the Korean War. He was 25 years old, in the prime of his career, when he joined the marines as a fighter pilot in 1942 and spent the next three years away from baseball, returning after the war in 1946.

Six years later, in 1952, Williams was recalled to active duty in the Korean War, and over the 1952 and 1953 seasons, when he was 34 and 35, Williams played only 43 games.

Adding his two tours of military duty together, Williams missed 727 possible games. If you extrapolate his career offensive numbers to include those missing games, you make an interesting discovery.

Based on his per-game averages for his career, in those missing games Williams would have been expected to hit 165 more home runs, to drive in 583 additional runs, to collect 843 extra hits, to add 166 more doubles to his total, and to collect 1,548 additional total bases.

What would those additions have meant? Williams would have ranked third all-time in career homers, first all-time in career RBIs, sixth all-time in career hits, fifth all-time in career doubles and second all-time in career total bases.

Using the same Rawlings scale of determining points for career rankings, Williams's revised total would have been 114 points—and he would have ranked as the greatest hitter of all time, one point ahead of Hank Aaron. Aaron's total would have decreased by two points because he would have moved down one spot in the lists for career RBI leaders and doubles leaders.

Those longtime observers who are not tied to strict statistical rankings, however, still consider Williams among the best hitters they ever saw.

"Did they tell me how to pitch to Williams?" asked Philadelphia A's pitcher Bobby Shantz one time. "Sure they did. They said he had no weaknesses, won't swing at a bad ball, had the best eyes in the business, and can kill you with one swing, he won't go after anything bad, but don't give him anything good."

That was exactly the kind of problem Williams created for American League pitchers ever since he

OPPOSITE: Ted Williams ended his baseball career with a .344 lifetime average. (John G. Zimmerman/Time Life Pictures/Getty Images)

"Williams was the most remarkable hitter I ever saw. I never saw a hitter who could swing as late as he did and hit the ball as good."

—Yankees catcher Bill Dickey

joined the Red Sox in 1939. As a 21-year-old rookie, he hit .322 with 31 homers and 145 RBIs.

Williams had signed with the Red Sox after joining the San Diego Padres of the Pacific Coast League in his hometown after graduating from high school. He was originally a left-handed pitcher, but he soon switched to the outfield and was in the majors three years later.

Williams was far from a one-year phenom, going on to win six batting titles and post a lifetime average of .344, winning his final title in 1958 at the age of 40. He became the last hitter in the majors to surpass the .400 mark when he hit .406 in 1941, and the facts about the last day of the season reveal a lot about Williams's character and his competitiveness.

Williams's average going into the final day of the season was .3995, which would round up to .400. Boston manager Joe Cronin asked Williams if he wanted to sit out or play in the doubleheader against the Philadelphia A's. The Yankees had long since clinched the pennant, so nothing else was riding on the outcome of the games. If Williams played, he likely would need three or four hits to keep his average at .400. Williams told Cronin he was playing.

He singled in his first at-bat and went on to get five more hits in the doubleheader, going a combined six for eight in the two games to finish the year at .406.

Williams had a love-hate relationship with the fans and was often perceived as cocky and arrogant. His poor relationship with the media likely cost him three MVP awards to go with the two he did win in 1946 and 1949.

Williams did not win the MVP in 1942 or 1947, despite winning the Triple Crown both seasons, losing out to the Yankees' Joe Gordon in 1942 and to Joe DiMaggio in 1947. He also lost out to DiMaggio and his 56-game hitting streak in 1941, the year he hit .406.

Williams topped the .300 mark in all but one of his 19 years in the majors and led the AL in homers four times, in RBIs three times, in total bases six times, and in runs scored six times. One negative statistic that always bothered him was that he only played in one World Series.

"Williams was the most remarkable hitter I ever saw," said Yankees catcher Bill Dickey. "I never saw a hitter who could swing as late as he did and hit the ball as good." Williams made one of the most dramatic finishes to his career that any hitter could imagine, hitting a home run in his final career at-bat at Fenway Park on September 28, 1960. Boston still had a three-game series to play in New York to conclude the season, but Williams announced after the game that he had played his final game.

ABOVE: Boston Red Sox legend Ted Williams may have had some fans crying foul, but there was no disputing his greatness on the field. (Hy Peskin/Time Life Pictures/Getty Images)

No. 25
Eddie Collins

If Eddie Collins had never even played baseball at the major league level, he would still be remembered for making a major contribution to the game. He was the scout responsible for the signing of Ted Williams and Bobby Doerr for the Boston Red Sox.

Williams turned out to be the 24th-ranked hitter of all time on the Rawlings scale of the game's greatest hitters—one spot ahead of Collins.

Collins was not only a great evaluator of talent after his playing career was over, he was more than a fair player himself. He collected a total of 30 points on the Rawlings scale, ranking 10th in career hits with 3,315 and 12th all-time in career triples.

A left-handed hitter, Collins came to the major leagues in 1906 as a 19-year-old shortstop with Connie Mack's Philadelphia A's. He moved to second base two years later and remained there for the rest of his career with the A's and the Chicago White Sox.

Collins actually made his major league debut while still a student at Columbia University. He played under the name of "Eddie Sullivan" in an attempt to retain his collegiate eligibility, but he was discovered and declared ineligible for his senior season at Columbia. He still remained in school and earned his degree.

The son of a lawyer who entered Columbia when he was only 16 years old, Collins always was considered one of the most intelligent players in the majors and reputedly was very adept at stealing signs from the other teams. He also was able to use his intelligence to make his team successful—he played in six World Series and helped his team win four world championships.

Collins was also a member of the 1919 White Sox, but he was never accused or implicated in the conspiracy to throw the Series to the Cincinnati Reds.

Collins was among the best players during the World Series, compiling 42 career hits and a .328 average during his six trips to the Series.

"For a man who could do anything—hit, field, run bases and play inside and brainy baseball—Collins stands at the top," said longtime rival Ty Cobb.

It was the presence of Cobb that cost Collins about the only title he was never able to achieve—a batting title. He had the misfortune of playing in Cobb's shadow as Cobb was winning 12 of 13 championships, but his World Series victories offset that disappointment.

A slash hitter who compiled a .333 career average, Collins hit better than .340 10 times and topped the .360 mark three times. He hit more than .300 for 18 seasons, topped by his career high of .369 in 1920. When he died in 1951, only three players in history had more hits than Collins—Cobb, Tris Speaker and Honus Wagner.

OPPOSITE: Baseball Hall of Fame member Eddie Collins finished his career with a .333 batting average. (AP/WWP)

"Eddie ain't superstitious. He just thinks it's unlucky not to get base hits."

Collins also led the league in runs three times and won three stolen base titles. An aggressive hitter, Collins most often hit a line-drive single, then stole second.

After leading the Athletics to the 1910, 1911 and 1913 world championships, Collins was sold to the White Sox for $100,000 as Mack broke up the Athletics after the 1914 season. At the time it was the most money ever paid for an individual player. He also won the World Series for the White Sox in 1917.

Collins continued to play until he was 43 years old, retiring in 1930. He also worked as a coach for Mack before moving into the front office of the Red Sox. He was elected to the Hall of Fame in 1939.

Collins had only small flaw as a player. He was superstitious, at least when it came time for him to come up to bat. He was a gum chewer, and as he walked to the plate, he took his chewing gum out of his mouth and placed it on top of his hat.

If he got two strikes on him, he called time and stepped out of the box, took the gum off his hat and put it back into his mouth and chewed vigorously. One opposing player didn't really view it as Collins being superstitious.

"Eddie ain't superstitious," the player said. "He just thinks it's unlucky not to get base hits."

OPPOSITE: Chicago White Sox second baseman Eddie Collins was one of the most intelligent players to ever don a baseball uniform. (AP/WWP)

100 >> RAWLINGS PRESENTS BIG STIX

If There Were a 26...

Any time a top 25 or similar list is compiled, the obvious question is: who just missed making the list? In this case, the answer is Reggie Jackson, who finished No. 26 in the Rawlings rankings.

Jackson is eighth all-time in career homers, 18th all-time in RBIs and 23rd all-time in total bases. He finished with 29 points on the Rawlings scale, one point less than the 25th-place finisher, Eddie Collins.

Jackson earned his nickname, "Mr. October," because of his World Series and postseason success, but it was his accomplishments during the regular season that gave him and his teammates a chance to play in that month.

In a 12-year span between 1971 and 1982, Jackson led the A's, Yankees and Angels to 10 division titles and five world championships. He won five consecutive division titles and three World Series with Oakland and two more world championships with the Yankees.

A power hitter who also set the career record for most strikeouts, Jackson hit 20 or more homers 13 times and either led or tied for the league lead in homers four times. He became the first hitter in history with 100 or more homers for three different teams: the A's, Yankees and Angels.

During his 21-year career, Jackson topped the 100 mark six times and played in 11 League Championship Series. He was named the American League MVP in 1963 and was elected to the Hall of Fame in his first year of eligibility, 1993.

Of all of Jackson's career homers, two that he is remembered for didn't even occur during the regular season. In the 1971 All-Star game at Detroit, Jackson hit a towering blast that struck a light tower above the roof in right center field at Tiger Stadium.

In the sixth and deciding game of the 1977 World Series, Jackson blasted three home runs to lead the Yankees to the victory over the Dodgers. The only other hitter in history to hit three home runs in a World Series game was Babe Ruth.

OPPOSITE: Reggie Jackson—"Mr. October"—nearly made the list of the top 25 biggest hitters. (Otto Greule/Getty Images)

Josh Gibson:
One of the Best

One hitter's name is missing from the top 25 Rawlings rankings, not because of an oversight or because he didn't belong. The name of Josh Gibson is missing because none of his hits came while he was wearing a major league uniform.

Those who saw Gibson perform in the Negro Leagues, however, insist he was one of the best hitters of all time.

"He had an eye like Ted Williams and the power of Babe Ruth," said Monte Irvin. "He hit to all fields."

Born in 1911, Gibson was a six-foot-one, 220-pound catcher who played with the Homestead Grays and the Pittsburgh Crawfords in the Negro Leagues from 1930 to 1946. Called the black Babe Ruth, stories persist of Gibson's legendary power.

He reportedly hit balls out of several major league stadiums, including Yankee Stadium, the Polo Grounds, Comiskey Park and Forbes Field. It has been reported that he hit 75 home runs in a season, and some analysts have computed his career home run total at 962, although both totals also are believed to include home runs that were hit in exhibition games and against semipro competition.

Gibson and Pittsburgh teammate Buck Leonard reportedly were candidates to be signed by major league teams prior to Jackie Robinson's signing with the Brooklyn Dodgers.

In 1939, the Pirates wanted to give both Gibson and Leonard tryouts but later changed their minds, some believe because of lobbying efforts by the owners of other major league teams who were committed to keeping the major leagues for whites only.

A few years later, the Washington Senators reportedly wanted to sign both Gibson and Leonard, not only to improve their club but also as a means of boosting attendance, but again were talked out of the idea by other owners.

Gibson's inability to play in the major leagues was cited by many observers as one of the reasons for his early death. Gibson was only 35 years old when he died of a cerebral hemorrhage in 1947.

OPPOSITE: Josh Gibson was known as the black Babe Ruth. (Photo provided by The Mark Reuben Gallery)

History of Rawlings

From a humble beginning more than 100 years ago, the Rawlings Sporting Goods Co. has grown to a giant in the industry.

George Rawlings and Charles Scudder opened a small retail sporting goods store in 1898 in St. Louis, never envisioning that their company would one day become one of the leading team sports equipment manufacturers in the world.

Rawlings was a well known local sporting goods figure in St. Louis, but his stay with the new company was brief. He left the company in 1906 and died shortly thereafter, but the name of the company remained the same.

In that same year, Rawlings outfitted the St. Louis Cardinals' baseball team with both home and road uniforms for the first time.

By 1907, the company had already grown to the point where it had expanded its offices, especially fueled by the sale of baseball equipment, and a decision was made to sell the retail operation and concentrate entirely on the manufacture of athletic equipment. One of the company's biggest areas of production was for "Football Armor Clothing" developed to protect the shoulders, collarbone and shoulder blades of football players. That equipment later came to be known as shoulder pads.

The same year, Rawlings obtained its first contract to supply baseballs to an organized professional league, the Texas State League.

A major obstacle had to be overcome two years later when the company's plant and offices were destroyed in a fire. Temporary production was set up while a new three-story building was built.

Business continued, and actually the onset of World War I turned out to provide a major boost to the company.

In a 1948 book commemorating the 50th anniversary of Rawlings, Bob Burnes wrote, "During World War I the government saw the necessity and benefits of athletics in the Service Training Programs and began a system of physical training for men in the service, which essentially was the beginning of a tremendous increase in the popularity of all sports. This keener interest for participation in sports survived after the 1918 Armistice, spread rapidly through many channels, and stimulated widespread sports activities in elementary and high schools.

"The growing development of athletics brought an increased demand for Rawlings equipment. This continued increase in sales and production, plus national recognition as a quality line, necessitated further expansion of manufacturing facilities."

OPPOSITE: Cofounder George Rawlings (Photo provided by Rawlings Sporting Goods Company, Inc.®)

The increase in business prompted the addition of another floor to the company's plant and the erection of another three-story building nearby. New machinery was installed, and the Rawlings plant became the model of the industry.

One of the most important days in the history of Rawlings came in 1920, when Bill Doak, a pitcher for the Cardinals, dropped by the company's offices to suggest how the standardized baseball gloves of the day could be improved. Those suggestions led Rawlings to develop a glove that became a standard for the industry.

The company was able to withstand the stock market crash of 1929 and the national depression, and in the late 1930s it received an increase in business because of its development of the equipment worn by army personnel, including helmets and other tank protective gear.

Personnel was increased approximately 40 percent to meet the production requirements of the war effort, as well as the continuing increase in demand for athletic equipment.

"The combined efforts of the plant personnel were rewarded on November 9, 1943 . . . when the company was awarded the first Army-Navy E made to the manufacturers of athletic goods," Burnes wrote. "This coveted honor was accepted by the management as recognition of the unstinted work and effort on the part of the employees."

ABOVE: Cardinal pitcher Bill Doak helped revolutionize the baseball glove. (Photo provided by Rawlings Sporting Goods Company, Inc.®)

The president of the company, Mason Scudder, said at the awards ceremony, "There have been many occasions when the Quartermaster Corps has called us for a particular job in a particular hurry, and while it required working long hours, through weekends and holidays, the men and women stayed on until the job was through."

Throughout the years, Rawlings has continued to have that same philosophy, which in turn has produced great success. There have been numerous innovations in the design of baseball gloves and mitts over the years. More major-leaguers today use Rawlings gloves than any other manufacturer, and since 1957, the company has been identified with fielding excellence by awarding a Gold Glove to the best fielders at each position.

Rawlings also has been the official and exclusive supplier of baseballs for the major leagues since 1977, including the baseballs used in the All-Star game and the World Series.

In addition to supplying the baseballs for every game and the gloves for a majority of major leagues, Rawlings also has for many years been the supplier of bats for a large number of major-leaguers.

Rawlings, through its ownership of Adirondack, is the second largest bat manufacturer for the major leagues, with about 30 percent of the players using their brand of bats. Some of the players who have used their bats over the years include Hank Aaron, Willie Mays, Mickey Mantle, Mark McGwire and Tony Gwynn.

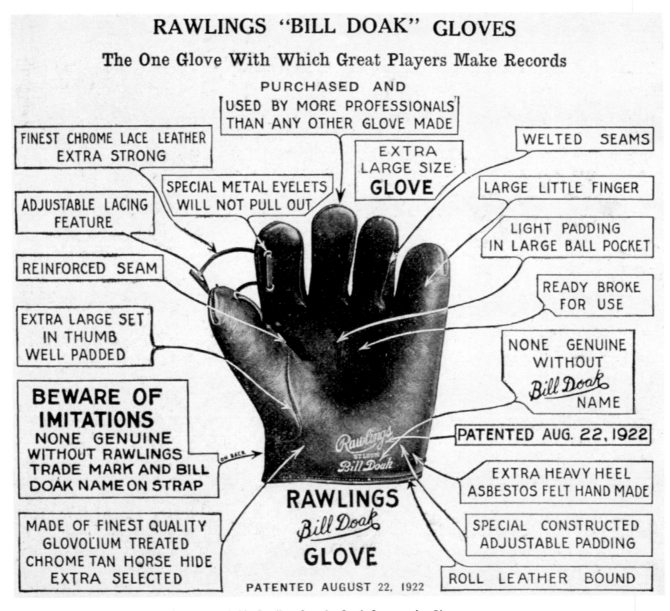

RAWLINGS "BILL DOAK" GLOVES

The One Glove With Which Great Players Make Records

PURCHASED AND USED BY MORE PROFESSIONALS THAN ANY OTHER GLOVE MADE

FINEST CHROME LACE LEATHER EXTRA STRONG

EXTRA LARGE SIZE GLOVE

WELTED SEAMS

ADJUSTABLE LACING FEATURE

SPECIAL METAL EYELETS WILL NOT PULL OUT

LARGE LITTLE FINGER

LIGHT PADDING IN LARGE BALL POCKET

REINFORCED SEAM

READY BROKE FOR USE

EXTRA LARGE SET IN THUMB WELL PADDED

NONE GENUINE WITHOUT *Bill Doak* NAME

BEWARE OF IMITATIONS NONE GENUINE WITHOUT RAWLINGS TRADE MARK AND BILL DOAK NAME ON STRAP

ON BACK

PATENTED AUG. 22, 1922

EXTRA HEAVY HEEL ASBESTOS FELT HAND MADE

MADE OF FINEST QUALITY GLOVOLIUM TREATED CHROME TAN HORSE HIDE EXTRA SELECTED

SPECIAL CONSTRUCTED ADJUSTABLE PADDING

ROLL LEATHER BOUND

RAWLINGS *Bill Doak* GLOVE

PATENTED AUGUST 22, 1922

ABOVE: Rawlings "Bill Doak" glove. (Photo provided by Rawlings Sporting Goods Company, Inc.®)

Rawlings Bat Maker Profile: Bill Steele

When Reggie Jackson hit his towering home run above the right field roof at Tiger Stadium in Detroit in the 1971 All-Star game, Bill Steele felt a small sense of pride.

Jackson was using one of the first bats that Steele had made since moving into the professional department at Adirondack's plant in Dolgeville, New York. The blast brought a smile to Steele's face.

More than 30 years later, Steele still marvels at the hitting ability of major-leaguers and revels in the small role he believes he has in their success.

Steele has been working for Adirondack—now owned by Rawlings—since 1969 and has been in the professional department almost as long. He continued to make Jackson's bats for the remainder of Jackson's career. Another home run hitter who relied on Steele over the years was Mark McGwire, who was using Steele's bats when he broke Roger Maris's single-season home run record in 1998.

As Steele has learned over the years, every major league player has his own peculiarities about what he wants in his bat. He has specific calculations for the length, weight, handle diameter and barrel diameter of the bat.

"With Mark, we had to get the knob just right," Steele says. "He wrapped his pinkie down below the knob, and it had to feel just right to him. Willie McCovey did the same thing."

The biggest change Steele has witnessed over the years is that the average bat has become lighter. Before Steele's days as a bat maker, Babe Ruth was known for using a 36-inch bat that weighed 42 ounces. During the 1970s, most bats were about 34 inches long and weighed between 32 and 33 ounces.

The average bat today of a major leaguer is 33 to 34 inches long and weighs between 30 and 31 ounces, Steele said. The reason is that hitters believe a lighter bat will allow them to generate greater bat speed, which they believe is the key to being a successful hitter.

Adirondack provides bats to more than 100 current major-leaguers. A player, on average, will go through about 120 bats in a season, Steele said. The biggest request he gets from a player is to make the bat's handle as thin as possible.

"The smaller the handle, the harder the bat is to make," Steele said. "It doesn't spin as true. I don't make handles that are smaller than 29/32nds of an inch. I don't think it is safe."

He once had a player ask him to make a bat that weighed only 28 ounces, and Steele tried but couldn't do it. "It just didn't look right," he said.

The player's goal, of course, was to be able to

Photo/imaging by Kenneth J. O'Brien

generate more bat speed because the bat was lighter. "The players keep getting bigger and bigger and the bats keep getting lighter and lighter," he said.

When the handle is too thin, the bat is easier to break, Steele said.

Steele does not get upset when he is watching a game and sees one of his bats break, unless it shatters and parts of the bat fly all over the field and sometimes into the stands. He worries about someone getting hurt by being struck by a piece of the bat.

"Bats break; it's part of the game," Steele said. "I look at it like I will be in business for another day."

Steele originally intended to work in the bat factory only as a summer job, but the longer he stayed the more he liked it, and his love of baseball helped launch that part-time job into a career.

The biggest change he has seen over the years is that when he began, all of the professionals' bats were made by hand. Now they are made by machine, except for the final sanding stage.

When he began, almost all of the major-leaguers' bats were made from ash. Now only about 75 percent come from ash, the others from maple, which has become more popular in the last few years. Ash is lighter than maple, Steele said, but he still believes it is better

wood for making a bat. Because maple weighs more, more of the wood has to be removed to make a bat out of maple than to make a bat of comparable size and weight out of ash.

"More and more people are wanting maple because it is a little harder, but not as much as everybody thinks it is," Steele said.

In all, the Adirondack factory turns out about 450,000 bats a year, of which only about 22,000 wind up in the hands of major league players. The rest go to the minor leagues, colleges, high schools and other amateur leagues.

The best part of Steele's job, he said, comes each spring when it is time to head to Florida and Arizona to meet with the major league players and discuss their bat orders. He can sit and talk hitting for hours.

"I love baseball," he said. "I played it and I watch it. I live for spring every year. A lot of people think I have a dream job, and it's true. As I get older it does become more of a job, but I look forward to spring training. I get to see the people I watch on TV and meet them and talk to them.

"I learn a lot about my job talking to hitters about hitting. The players know more about their bats than anybody else, and they love to talk about it."

The Bat-Making Process

Making a baseball bat is easy, right? The people who work at the Rawlings/Adirondack bat factory in Dolgeville, New York are convinced that you would have a different answer after taking a closer look at all that goes into making one bat.

No matter if that bat is headed for a major-leaguer or into the hands of a 12-year-old Little Leaguer, a great deal of effort goes into making certain that bat is made correctly. The majority of the bats are made from Northern white ash, a tree that grows in New York and Pennsylvania.

Once a tree is cut down and the lumber shipped to the bat factory, the bark is stripped from the log and the log is cut into 40-inch sections, called bolts. Each bolt is then split lengthwise into wedge-shaped pieces of wood called splits.

The splits are placed on a lathe, which turns them into 3 1/8-inch billets. Those billets are then stacked on pallets to dry. It takes about 30 days for the moisture content of the billets to reach the desired 10 percent. From that point, it takes about 35 minutes to complete the manufacturing of each individual bat. Each billet is then cut to a uniform length of 37 inches, and the lathe trims each bat to a diameter of two inches.

Numerous weighing, grading and inspection operations eliminate any pieces of wood that are of inferior quality. One of the biggest items checked is the quality of the grain lines, which should be as straight as possible as they run from the barrel of the bat to the handle.

The billets are then placed back on the lathe, where they are turned to the desired length and shape for each individual bat. Most are made into generic models, but each major-leaguer has his own specific dimensions for the length and weight of his bat.

Each bat then goes through a series of sanding operations to ensure the surface is smooth. The knobs on either end of the bat, called "dead wood," are used to hold the raw material in the lathes, then removed with a saw and the ends finished by sanding.

In the finishing operation, the bat is flame-treated with a natural gas-produced flame lightly passed over the outside of the surface of the bat. This hardens the bat surface and accentuates the grain structure of the wood. Next, a colored wood filler is applied, which serves a twofold purpose: one, to fill the open pores of the wood, and two, to give the bat an attractive color.

After the filler is dry, the code number indicating the model and length is stamped on the knob end of the bat, followed by the Rawlings/Adirondack trademark. It is then personalized with the ballplayer's signature. The trademark is always stamped on the flat side of the grain so that the bat, when held properly with the trademark up, will make contact with the ball on the edge of the grain where the bat has maximum strength.

The bat is almost complete. All that is left is to add the famous "Pro Ring" to the handle, followed by two coats of lacquer finish. The bats are then ready to be shipped, whether to a major-leaguer or to a Little Leaguer dreaming of one day being the next major league star.

ABOVE: A worker places a wooden baseball bat on the assembly line at the Rawlings/Adirondack bat factory in Dolgeville, New York, in this June 1956 photo. (AP/WWP)

Five Biggest Hits

Great moments in history are remembered by time and place—where you were and what you were doing at the specific moment that history occurred. Such is the case with dramatic hits in baseball as well—fans remember if they were in the stadium, watching on television or listening on the radio.

Some times a moment caps a dramatic streak—such as was the case when Mark McGwire finally broke Roger Maris's home run record with his 62nd home run in 1998 and Pete Rose finally passing Ty Cobb's record and becoming the all-time hits leader in baseball history.

Other moments offer no warning and become monumental because of their unpredictability and drama. That was true the night Joe Carter won the 1993 World Series with a three-run homer, the night Kirk Gibson hobbled off the bench to hit a home run in the 1988 World Series, and the day Bill Mazeroski's homer won the 1960 World Series.

Even though McGwire hit eight additional homers after his 62nd home run in 1998, and even though Sammy Sosa also surpassed Maris's record—and even though Barry Bonds broke McGwire's record only three years later—there is no doubt McGwire's passing Maris ranks as one of the biggest hits of all time.

On September 8, 1998, the Cardinals were playing the Cubs at Busch Stadium. In his second at-bat against Steve Trachsel and with Maris's children watching from behind the Cardinals' dugout, McGwire connected on what turned out to be his shortest homer of the season, just clearing the left field wall. Maris's record, which had stood for 37 years, had been broken.

The celebration lasted for several minutes, and included McGwire hugging Sosa, who trotted in from right field, and McGwire going into the stands to shake hands and receive hugs from Maris's children.

A similar celebration had occurred on September 11, 1985, at Riverfront Stadium in Cincinnati. Pete Rose, a native of Cincinnati, had returned to his hometown team the previous year as his pursuit of Cobb's all-time hits record continued. He had tied Cobb's mark of 4,191 hits two days earlier in Chicago, then went zero for four in the next game.

Facing the Padres' Eric Show in the bottom of the first inning, Rose lined a 2-1 pitch into left center field for a single to break his tie with Cobb, who had held the record for 57 years. Rose broke down as he stood at first base, being hugged by his son and his teammates while the sellout crowd gave him a seven-minute ovation.

Those two big hits were predictable—if not the exact time and place, at least the probability that they would happen sometime. Other big hits offered no such warning.

OPPOSITE: Mark McGwire breaks the record of 61 home runs set by Roger Maris. (AP/WWP)

ABOVE: Joe Carter celebrates his World Series–winning home run. (Rick Stewart/Getty Images)

That was certainly true on October 23, 1993, when Joe Carter stepped to the plate for the Toronto Blue Jays with one out in the bottom of the ninth inning in Game 6 of the World Series at Skydome. The Blue Jays trailed the Phillies 6-5, and despite having runners on first and second, they appeared headed for a loss that would force a deciding seventh game the following night.

Instead, Carter sent a 2-2 pitch from Mitch Williams into the left field stands, giving Toronto the win and making the Blue Jays the first team since the 1977-78 Yankees to win back-to-back world championships.

It was only the second time in history a World Series game had ended on a come-from-behind home run.

The first time that had happened was five years earlier, on October 15, 1988, in Game 1 of the World Series between the Los Angeles Dodgers and Oakland A's. Oakland led 4-3 and had ace closer Dennis Eckersley on the mound. With a runner on and two out, manager Tommy Lasorda sent a hobbling Kirk Gibson out to pinch hit for pitcher Alejandro Pena.

Gibson had spent the previous eight innings in the training room, beset by leg injuries, but he stood at the plate and hit a 3-2 pitch into the right field seats

OPPOSITE: Kirk Gibson raises his fist in triumph after his miracle home run to win Game 1 of the 1988 World Series. (AP/WWP)

to give the Dodgers a 5-4 win. Broadcaster Jack Buck, working the game on radio, delivered an epic call by saying "I don't believe what I just saw," as Gibson slowly made his way around the bases. The Dodgers went on to win the Series in five games.

One of the most dramatic home runs in World Series history came on October 13, 1960, in Game 7 of the Series between the Yankees and Pirates at Forbes Field in Pittsburgh. With the score tied at nine, Bill Mazeroski led off the bottom of the ninth against Ralph Terry and delivered the game-winning blast that made the Pirates the world champions, despite the fact the Yankees scored 28 more runs in the Series and set a record with a .338 team batting average.

Certainly people remember where they were for other dramatic hits as well—Bucky Dent's home run off Mike Torrez in a 1978 playoff game that put the Yankees into the playoffs instead of Boston; Carlton Fisk's game-winning homer in the 12th inning of Game 6 of the 1975 World Series between the Red Sox and Reds, and Bobby Thomson's pennant-winning homer for the Giants in the 1951 playoff game against the Dodgers.

OPPOSITE: Bill Mazeroski is mobbed by fans after his home run won the World Series for the Pirates. (AP/WWP)

Top Five Active Hitters

While Barry Bonds and Rafael Palmeiro are clearly the top active hitters in the game today, there are five more who definitely need to be saluted for their career accomplishments.

The highest-ranked hitters after those two are Fred McGriff, Rickey Henderson, Roberto Alomar, Sammy Sosa and Andres Galarraga. They represent a wide range of hitting characteristics, with McGriff and Sosa being known primarily as home run hitters and Henderson and Alomar more as contact hitters. Galarraga is a combination of the two.

McGriff, who finished the 2003 season as a member of the San Francisco Giants, is fourth among active players in home runs, third in RBIs, fifth in hits, 10th in doubles and fourth in total bases. He ranks 21st in career home runs with 491, only nine away from becoming the 20th member of the 500-home run club.

McGriff has hit 30 or more homers eight times in his career and six times has topped the 100-RBI mark. He also leads all active major-leaguers by having hit at least one home run in 37 different stadiums.

Henderson finished the 2003 season with the Dodgers after playing part of the year in an independent minor league. He leads active major-leaguers in hits, and his total of 3,055 ranks him 20th on the all-time list. The 1990 MVP with the Oakland A's also ranks fourth among current players in doubles and is third in total bases.

Alomar might be the most surprising player on the list, because he is not a power hitter and does not attract as much attention for his hitting ability. He ranks third among active players in hits with 2,679 and also is third among active players in triples, fifth in career doubles and eighth in career total bases. He has signed with the Arizona Diamondbacks for the 2004 season.

Sosa might be the most talked-about player on the list of the top active hitters, because of his popularity and his home run success with the Chicago Cubs. He is second to Bonds among active players in career homers with 539, 10th all-time, and he would appear to have a good chance of becoming only the fifth player ever to top the 600-homer mark for his career.

Sosa is fourth among current players in RBIs and fifth in total bases. He is the only player in history to hit 60 or more homers three times and has hit 40 or more homers for six consecutive years and driven in 100 or more runs for nine consecutive years. All but 29 of his career homers have come with the Cubs, leaving him only three homers away from breaking the team's record of 512 set by Ernie Banks.

For the 10-year span between 1994 and 2003, Sosa hit 469 homers, setting a major league record for most homers in a 10-year span. The previous record had been 467, set by Babe Ruth between 1920 and 1929.

ABOVE: Fred McGriff (Rick Stewart/Getty Images) BELOW: Rickey Henderson (Donald Miralle/Getty Images)

Galarraga finished the 2003 season with the Giants, the fourth season he played in the majors after missing the 1999 season while being treated for lymphoma, a form of cancer, which many people thought would end his career. He ranks ninth among active players in career homers with 398, is fifth in RBIs, eighth in career hits, ninth in doubles and sixth in total bases.

During the peak years of his career, Galarraga hit 30 or more homers for five consecutive years, drove in 100 or more runs for five consecutive years and hit .300 or better in eight seasons.

Even though he has played only three seasons, not long enough to qualify him for any career leading categories, the Cardinals' Albert Pujols has enjoyed the fastest start to a career of any hitter in baseball history and, if he can continue at a similar pace, definitely will crack this list—and perhaps the top 25 all-time list—in the not too distant future.

Top Five World Series Hitters

Starting with Babe Ruth's first year as a member of the New York Yankees, through the last season of Mickey Mantle's career in 1968, the Bronx Bombers dominated baseball like no team before or since.

During that 49-year span, the Yankees appeared in the World Series 29 times, winning 20 world championships.

There are some explanations for that incredible success. There were fewer teams in the major leagues then; there were no extra rounds of playoffs, with a team only having to win the pennant before moving directly to the World

ABOVE: Yogi Berra (Hulton Archive/Getty Images)

Series; and one additional, very obvious factor—the Yankees simply had better players than any other team.

It is no surprise that the top five hitters of all time in World Series competition using the Rawlings scale all played the majority of their careers with the Yankees—Yogi Berra, Mantle, Lou Gehrig, Ruth and Joe DiMaggio.

Berra ranks as the greatest World Series hitter of all time on the Rawlings scale, finishing with 45.5 points. He has the most World Series hits in history, 71, is third all-time in homers with 12, is second in RBIs, second in total bases and tied for the most doubles.

During Berra's career, the three-time MVP spent 17 full years with the Yankees—and played in 14 World Series. He earned 10 world championship rings, the most in history.

Mantle also had unprecedented success in the World Series, appearing in the Fall Classic 12 times in a 14-year span between 1951 and 1964, winning seven championships. He finished second in the Rawlings rankings with 39 points. He has hit the most home runs in the World Series, 18, has the most RBIs, has the most total bases and is second to Berra in career hits.

OPPOSITE: Mickey Mantle (Hulton Archive/Getty Images)

Mickey Mantle

Mantle, like Berra a three-time MVP, was responsible for the Yankees appearing in so many World Series because of his success in the regular season. He led the American League in homers four times and won the Triple Crown in 1956 despite his painful battles with knee injuries.

Gehrig and Ruth both had enough success, and long enough careers, to make the top 25 rankings for their regular-season performances. Ruth finished in a tie for 10th on the all-time list of greatest hitters, and Gehrig finished in 18th place. They continued that success in the World Series, with Gehrig finishing as the third best hitter in World Series play with 26.5 points on the Rawlings scale, while Ruth finished fourth with 24.33 points.

Gehrig is tied for fifth all-time with 10 World Series homers, is third in RBIs, fourth in total bases, tied for sixth in doubles and ninth in career Series hits.

Ruth is second to Mantle with 15 World Series homers, fourth in RBIs, third in total bases, and tied for 10th in hits.

The other Yankees player completing the top five hitters in the history of the World Series is DiMaggio, who played in 10 Series and earned nine championships during a 13-year career. He missed three seasons while serving in the military.

DiMaggio finished with 22 points on the Rawlings scale. He is fourth in career hits, tied for seventh in career homers, fifth in RBIs and fifth in total bases.

Also a three-time MVP, DiMaggio is best known for his record 56-game hitting streak in 1941, but he

ABOVE: Lou Gehrig (AP/WWP)

also won two home run titles and two batting championships during his Hall of Fame career.

The top two non-Yankees on the list of the Rawlings rankings of the greatest hitters in World Series history tied for sixth with 20 points—Duke Snider and Frankie Frisch.

OPPOSITE: Joe DiMaggio (Hulton Archive/Getty Images)

By the Numbers

Top 25 Overall Hitters

Name	Points
1. Hank Aaron	115
2. Ty Cobb	112
3. Stan Musial	99
4. Tris Speaker	79
5. Willie Mays	78
6. Honus Wagner	74
7. Carl Yastrzemski	73
8. (tie) Pete Rose	69
Babe Ruth	69
10. Eddie Murray	66
11. Cap Anson	54
12. (tie) Barry Bonds	49
Frank Robinson	49
14. Cal Ripken	47
15. George Brett	43
16. Paul Waner	41.5
17. Jimmie Foxx	41
18. Lou Gehrig	40
19. Dave Winfield	39.5
20. Paul Molitor	37.5
21. Rafael Palmeiro	35.5
22. (tie) Mel Ott	34
Nap Lajoie	34
24. Ted Williams	32.5
25. Eddie Collins	30

Top 25 Home Runs

Name	Homers
1. Hank Aaron	755
2. Babe Ruth	714
3. Willie Mays	660
4. Barry Bonds	658
5. Frank Robinson	586
6. Mark McGwire	583
7. Harmon Killebrew	573
8. Reggie Jackson	563
9. Mike Schmidt	548
10. Sammy Sosa	539
11. Mickey Mantle	536
12. Jimmie Foxx	534
13. Rafael Palmeiro	528
14. (tie) Willie McCovey	521
Ted Williams	521
16. (tie) Ernie Banks	512
Eddie Mathews	512
18. Met Ott	511
19. Eddie Murray	504
20. Lou Gehrig	493
21. Fred McGriff	491
22. Ken Griffey Jr.	481
23. (tie) Stan Musial	475
Willie Stargell	475
25. Dave Winfield	465

Top 25 Hits

Name	Hits
1. Pete Rose	4,256
2. Ty Cobb	4,189
3. Hank Aaron	3,771
4. Stan Musial	3,630
5. Tris Speaker	3,514
6. Carl Yastrzemski	3,419
7. Cap Anson	3,418
8. Honus Wagner	3,415
9. Paul Molitor	3,319
10. Eddie Collins	3,315
11. Willie Mays	3,283
12. Eddie Murray	3,255
13. Nap Lajoie	3,242
14. Cal Ripken	3,184
15. George Brett	3,154
16. Paul Waner	3,152
17. Robin Yount	3,142
18. Tony Gwynn	3,141
19. Dave Winfield	3,110
20. Rickey Henderson	3,055
21. Rod Carew	3,053
22. Lou Brock	3,023
23. Wade Boggs	3,010
24. Al Kaline	3,007
25. Roberto Clemente	3,000

Top 25 RBIs

Name	Total
1. Hank Aaron	2,297
2. Babe Ruth	2,213
3. Cap Anson	2,076
4. Lou Gehrig	1,995
5. Stan Musial	1,951
6. Ty Cobb	1,937
7. Jimmie Foxx	1,922
8. Eddie Murray	1,917
9. Willie Mays	1,903
10. Mel Ott	1,860
11. Carl Yastrzemski	1,844
12. Ted Williams	1,839
13. Dave Winfield	1,833
14. Al Simmons	1,827
15. Frank Robinson	1,812
16. Barry Bonds	1,742
17. Honus Wagner	1,732
18. Reggie Jackson	1,702
19. Cal Ripken	1,695
20. Rafael Palmeiro	1,687
21. Tony Perez	1,652
22. Ernie Banks	1,636
23. Harold Baines	1,628
24. Goose Goslin	1,609
25. Nap Lajoie	1,599

Top 25 Doubles

Name	Total
1. Tris Speaker	792
2. Pete Rose	746
3. Stan Musial	725
4. Ty Cobb	724
5. George Brett	665
6. Nap Lajoie	657
7. Carl Yastrzemski	646
8. Honus Wagner	640
9. Hank Aaron	624
10. (tie) Paul Molitor	605
Paul Waner	605
12. Cal Ripken	603
13. Robin Yount	583
14. Cap Anson	581
15. Wade Boggs	578
16. Charlie Gehringer	574
17. Eddie Murray	560
18. (tie) Tony Gwynn	543
Rafael Palmeiro	543
20. Harry Heilmann	542
21. Rogers Hornsby	541
22. (tie) Joe Medwick	540
Dave Winfield	540
24. Al Simmons	539
25. Barry Bonds	536

Top 25 Triples

Name	Total
1. Sam Crawford	309
2. Ty Cobb	295
3. Honus Wagner	252
4. Jake Beckley	243
5. Roger Connor	233
6. Tris Speaker	222
7. Fred Clarke	220
8. Dan Brouthers	205
9. Joe Kelly	194
10. Paul Waner	191
11. Bid McPhee	188
12. Eddie Collins	187
13. Ed Delahanty	185
14. Sam Rice	184
15. (tie) Jesse Burkett	182
Ed Konetchy	182
Edd Raush	182
18. Buck Ewing	178
19. (tie) Rabbit Maranville	177
Stan Musial	177
21. Harry Stovey	174
22. Goose Goslin	173
23. (tie) Tommy Leach	172
Zach Wheat	172
25. Rogers Hornsby	169

Top 25 Total Bases

Name	Total
1. Hank Aaron	6,856
2. Stan Musial	6,134
3. Willie Mays	6,066
4. Ty Cobb	5,854
5. Babe Ruth	5,793
6. Pete Rose	5,752
7. Carl Yastrzemski	5,539
8. Eddie Murray	5,397
9. Frank Robinson	5,373
10. Barry Bonds	5,253
11. Dave Winfield	5,221
12. Cal Ripken	5,168
13. Tris Speaker	5,101
14. Lou Gehrig	5,060
15. George Brett	5,044
16. Mel Ott	5,041
17. Rafael Palmeiro	4,983
18. Jimmie Foxx	4,956
19. Ted Williams	4,884
20. Honus Wagner	4,862
21. Paul Molitor	4,854
22. Al Kaline	4,852
23. Reggie Jackson	4,834
24. Andre Dawson	4,787
25. Robin Yount	4,730

Top 7 Total Active Players

Name	Points
1. Barry Bonds	53
2. Rafael Palmeiro	45
3. Fred McGriff	29
4. Rickey Henderson	27
5. Roberto Alomar	25
6. Sammy Sosa	22
7. Andres Galarraga	18

Top 10 Active Home Runs

Name	Total
1. Barry Bonds	658
2. Sammy Sosa	539
3. Rafael Palmeiro	528
4. Fred McGriff	491
5. Ken Griffey Jr.	481
6. Juan Gonzalez	429
7. Jeff Bagwell	419
8. Frank Thomas	418
9. Andres Galarraga	398
10. Jim Thome	381

Top 10 Active Hits

Name	Total
1. Rickey Henderson	3,055
2. Rafael Palmeiro	2,780
3. Roberto Alomar	2,679

4.	Barry Bonds	2,595
5.	Fred McGriff	2,477
6.	Craig Biggio	2,461
7.	Julio Franco	2,358
8.	Andres Galarraga	2,370
9.	Barry Larkin	2,240
10.	Steve Finley	2,166

Top 10 Active RBIs

Name		Total
1.	Barry Bonds	1,742
2.	Rafael Palmeiro	1,687
3.	Fred McGriff	1,543
4.	Sammy Sosa	1,450
5.	Andres Galarraga	1,423
6.	Jeff Bagwell	1,421
7.	Frank Thomas	1,390
8.	Juan Gonzalez	1,387
9.	Ken Griffey Jr.	1,384
10.	Gary Sheffield	1,232

Top 10 Active Doubles

Name		Total
1.	Rafael Palmeiro	543
2.	Barry Bonds	536
3.	Craig Biggio	517
4.	Rickey Henderson	510
5.	Roberto Alomar	498
6.	Edgar Martinez	494
7.	John Olerud	473
8.	Jeff Bagwell	455
9.	Andres Galarraga	444
10.	Fred McGriff	438

Top 10 Active Triples

Name		Total
1.	Steve Finley	108
2.	Kenny Lofton	86
3.	Roberto Alomar	78
4.	Barry Bonds	74

5.	Barry Larkin	73
6.	Jose Offerman	69
7.	Johnny Damon	68
8.	Jay Bell	67
9.	Rickey Henderson	66
10.	Ellis Burks	63

Top 10 Active Total Bases

Name		Total
1.	Barry Bonds	5,253
2.	Rafael Palmeiro	4,983
3.	Rickey Henderson	4,588
4.	Fred McGriff	4,436
5.	Sammy Sosa	4,121
6.	Andres Galarraga	4,032
7.	Ken Griffey Jr.	3,977
8.	Roberto Alomar	3,951
9.	Jeff Bagwell	3,909
10.	Frank Thomas	3,752

Top 5 World Series Leaders

Name		Points
1.	Yogi Berra	45.5
2.	Mickey Mantle	39
3.	Lou Gehrig	26.5
4.	Babe Ruth	24.33
5.	Joe DiMaggio	22

Top 10 World Series Home Runs

Name		Total
1.	Mickey Mantle	18
2.	Babe Ruth	15
3.	Yogi Berra	12
4.	Duke Snider	11
5.	(tie) Lou Gehrig	10
	Reggie Jackson	10
7.	(tie) Joe DiMaggio	8
	Frank Robinson	8
	Bill Skowron	8
10.	(tie) Hank Bauer	7

Goose Goslin	7
Gil McDougald	7

Top 10 World Series Hits

Name	Total
1. Yogi Berra	71
2. Mickey Mantle	59
3. Frankie Frisch	58
4. Joe DiMaggio	54
5. (tie) Hank Bauer	46
Pee Wee Reese	46
7. (tie) Gil McDougald	45
Phil Rizzuto	45
9. (tie) Eddie Collins	42
Elston Howard	42
Babe Ruth	42

Top 10 World Series RBI

Name	Total
1. Mickey Mantle	40
2. Yogi Berra	39
3. Lou Gehrig	35
4. Babe Ruth	33
5. Joe DiMaggio	30
6. Bill Skowron	29
7. Duke Snider	26
8. (tie) Hank Bauer	24
Bill Dickey	24
Reggie Jackson	24
Gil McDougald	24

Top 10 World Series Doubles

Name	Total
1. (tie) Yogi Berra	10
Frankie Frisch	10
3. (tie) Jack Barry	9
Pete Fox	9
Carl Furillo	9
6. (tie) Lou Gehrig	8
Lonnie Smith	8
Duke Snider	8
9. Five tied with 7	

Top 10 World Series Triples

Name	Total
1. (tie) Bobby Johnson	4
Tommy Leach	4
Tris Speaker	4
4. 14 tied with 3	

Top 10 World Series Total Bases

Name	Total
1. Mickey Mantle	123
2. Yogi Berra	117
3. Babe Ruth	96
4. Lou Gehrig	87
5. Joe DiMaggio	84
6. Duke Snider	79
7. Hank Bauer	75
8. (tie) Frankie Frisch	74
Reggie Jackson	74
10. Gil McDougald	72

Factoids

- The only player to hold the record for most home runs in a season for two different franchises is Jimmie Foxx, who hit 58 homers for the Philadelphia A's in 1932 and 50 home runs for the Boston Red Sox in 1938.

- The only two franchises that have never had a player hit 40 or more home runs in a season are the Kansas City Royals and Tampa Bay Devil Rays. Steve Balboni holds the Royals' record with 36 homers in 1985, and Jose Canseco has the Tampa record with 34 homers in 1999.

- The only teams that have never had a player lead his league in home runs for a season are Kansas City, Tampa Bay, Arizona, Florida, Houston and Montreal.

- The only players to hold their teams' records for both most home runs in a season and most hits in a season are Luis Gonzalez of Arizona, who hit 57 home runs in 2001 and recorded 206 hits in 1999, and Vladimir Guerrero of Montreal, who hit 44 home runs and recorded 206 hits in 2000.

- The only franchises that have never had a player lead his league in batting average for a season are Tampa Bay, Arizona, Florida, Houston, Milwaukee and the New York Mets.

- The only player to hold the record for most hits in a season for two franchises is Rogers Hornsby, who had 250 hits for the Cardinals in 1922 and 229 hits for the Chicago Cubs in 1929.

- The only franchises that have never had a player record 200 or more hits in a season are Tampa Bay and Florida. Randy Winn had 181 hits for Tampa in 2002, and Luis Castillo had 185 hits for Florida in 2002.

- Ty Cobb holds the record for the most consecutive years hitting .300—23 years.

- The career record for pinch hits is 173, set by Lenny Harris.

- Hank Aaron has the career record for most home runs for one club: the Braves, 733.

- The career record for most home runs by a second baseman is 275, set by Ryne Sandberg, the lowest total for any position except pitcher.

- Wes Ferrell has the career record for most home runs by a pitcher: 37.

- Rickey Henderson holds the record for most times leading off a game with a home run. He has done it 80 times.

- Hank Aaron has the record for the most 20-home run seasons in a career, 20, and the record for the most 30-home run seasons, 15.

- The career record for pinch-hit home runs is 20, set by Cliff Johnson.

- The record for most home runs hit in All-Star game competition is six, by Stan Musial.

- There have been only 13 .400-seasons in major league history, recorded by eight different hitters.

- The record for the longest consecutive hitting streak by a rookie is 34 games, set by San Diego's Benito Santiago in 1987.

- The record for most consecutive hits is 12, set by Pinky Higgins of the Red Sox in 1938 and tied by Walt Dropo of Detroit in 1952.

- The record for most consecutive games hitting a home run is eight. The record was set by Dale Long of the Pirates in 1956 and equaled by Don Mattingly of the Yankees in 1987 and Ken Griffey Jr. of the Mariners in 1993.

- There have been 12 games in major league history in which a hitter hit four home runs. Nine of those games were nine-inning games.

- Sammy Sosa of the Cubs tied the record for most two-home run games in a season in 1998 when he did it 11 times. The record had been set by Hank Greenberg of the Tigers in 1938.

- The record for most home runs in a game by one team is 10, set by Toronto on September 14, 1987. The National League record is nine, set by the Cincinnati Reds on September 4, 1999.

- The last American League pitcher to hit a home run in a game was Roric Harrison of Baltimore on October 3, 1972.

- The only players who hold their team's career records for most home runs, hits and RBIs are Hank Aaron (Braves), Luis Gonzalez (Diamondbacks), Robin Yount (Brewers), Mike Schmidt (Phillies), Stan Musial (Cardinals), Cal Ripken Jr. (Orioles), George Brett (Royals) and Fred McGriff (Devil Rays).

- The only member of the Anaheim Angels ever to lead the American League in hitting was Alex Johnson in 1970.

- The only member of the Chicago White Sox to ever lead the American League in RBIs was Dick Allen in 1972.

- The only member of the Texas Rangers ever to lead the American League in batting average was Julio Franco in 1991.

- Twelve of the 16 National League teams have seen their franchise record for most home runs in a season either broken or tied in the last eight seasons (since 1996). The only records older than 1996 are the Braves (Eddie Mathews, 47, 1953), Phillies (Mike Schmidt, 48, 1980), Pirates (Ralph Kiner, 54, 1949) and Reds (George Foster, 52, 1977).

- The New York Mets' record for most home runs in a season is 41, set by Todd Hundley in 1996.

- Only three teams in major league history (since 1900) have recorded 30 or more hits in one game—the Cleveland Indians had 33 on July 10, 1932; the Giants had 31 on June 9, 1901; and Milwaukee had 31 on August 28, 1992.

- Excluding the four expansion franchises added since 1993 (Colorado, Florida, Arizona and Tampa Bay), the Kansas City Royals are the only major league team to have been no-hit only once. Nolan Ryan pitched the only no-hitter against the Royals on May 15, 1973.

- The Philadelphia Phillies have been the victims of no-hitters more than any other franchise in major league history. Opponents have pitched 21 career no-hitters against the Phillies.